Power
Taiji

Power Taiji

強壯太極拳

Erle Montaigue
and Michael Babin

PALADIN PRESS
BOULDER, COLORADO

Also by Erle Montaigue:

Advanced Dim-Mak: The Finer Points of Death-Point Striking

Dim-Mak: Death-Point Striking

Dim-Mak's 12 Most Deadly Katas: Points of No Return

Encyclopedia of Dim-Mak: The Main Meridians (with Wally Simpson)

Encyclopedia of Dim-Mak: The Extra Meridians, Points, and More (with Wally Simpson)

Secrets of Dim-Mak: An Instructional Video

Ultimate Dim-Mak: How to Fight A Grappler and Win

Also by Michael Babin:

T'ai Chi Ch'uan: The Martial Side

Power Taiji
by Erle Montaigue and Michael Babin

Copyright © 1995 by Erle Montaigue and Michael Babin

ISBN 0-87364-846-3
Printed in the United States of America

Published by Paladin Press, a division of
Paladin Enterprises, Inc., P.O. Box 1307,
Boulder, Colorado 80306, USA.
(303) 443-7250

Direct inquires and/or orders to the above address.

Visit our Web site at www.paladin-press.com

contents

warning

Some of the techniques depicted in this book are extremely dangerous. It is not the intent of the author, publisher, or distributors of this book to encourage readers to attempt any of these techniques without proper professional supervision and training. Attempting to do so can result in severe injury or death. Do not attempt any of these techniques without the supervision of a certified instructor.

The author, publisher, and distributors of this book disclaim any liability from any damages or injuries of any type that a reader or user of information contained within this book may encounter from the use or misuse of said information. *This book is presented for academic study only.*

foreword

Martial arts are a Chinese national sport. They are also to be treasured by all people of the world. They are not governed by sex, age, location, seasons, or weapons. Because peoples of the world are now exchanging cultures and martial artists have similar interests, friendships of mutual benefit to all concerned are being formed.

The purpose of a martial art is to toughen your bones and muscles for self-defense and to improve your intelligence and mental attitude. Martial arts consist of both attack and defense, and these movements need to be placed in sequence to create a style. Taijiquan is one style of martial art. There are five different versions. The most popular versions in China are the Chen and Yang styles. The Yang style is very relaxed, smooth, and slow, with internal strength. It is suitable for all people, including the old, the weak, or those suffering from illness.

In May 1985, Erle Montaigue brought the Australian Taijiquan Boxing Association members to visit Yinchuan City in Ningxia to see the All-China National Wushu Competition. Master Montaigue gave a demonstration of his Yang-style taijiquan, which was very well received by the audience, and the local newspapers and television station interviewed him. He is well remembered by the Chinese people since this time.

I saw Master Montaigue's demonstration. His tui-sau (push-hands), qi development, and style were very professional and close to perfection. I appreciate his knowledge. I know Master Montaigue has introduced taijiquan to Australia and the Pacific region with excellent results.

I am one of the direct descendants to inherit the Yang-style taijiquan. I have written a book of 48 techniques, and I am also a Chinese taijiquan champion. Master Montaigue and I have built a very good friendship because of our mutual love of taijiquan and the fact that we are close to the same age [in terms of experience in taiji, not in literal years —Ed.]. Also, we both have beards and curly hair and have worked on films.

Our friendship is not only on a personal basis, however; my hope is that it will cement a friendship between Australia and China and group together to improve the standard of martial arts. I wish Master Montaigue every success in his business, and I wish Australia national success in taijiquan. I send my special regards to martial arts devotees throughout the world.

—MASTER WANG XIN-WU

Master Wang, of China, is the creator of the Peking 48 style of taijiquan.

preface

There are three main Chinese internal martial arts: hsinyiquan, bagwazhang, and taijiquan (t'ai chi ch'uan). The last is reputed to be the mother, the original source, of the other two.

What these three have in common with each other and with all great martial arts are methods whereby the body and mind are made strong and coordinated. From this perspective, *qi* (*ch'i,* or internal energy) cultivation is the most important aspect of one's taijiquan training.

Qi is our life force from conception, the very thing that holds our molecules together, an internal bioelectrical force. It stands to reason that if we have little of this force, or if the flow of qi is impeded, then we are not too healthy.

Taijiquan is a type of moving *qigong* (*ch'i kung*), which means "internal work" and involves specific physical postures and movements used in conjunction with certain breathing techniques. Using these as described in the coming chapters, we are able to build upon the qi we are born with (prenatal qi) and then make it flow benefically during our practice of the taijiquan form.

One of the primary aims of our taiji training is to augment our store of this energy so that our organs are literally bathed in life-giving qi. However, if we wish to then use qi for healing or martial purposes, then we must turn it into a refined form of energy called *jing.*

Every taijiquan posture causes the internal energy to flow through its corresponding organ, and so the whole traditional taiji form is made up of these postures, sequenced to allow this flow to happen without forcing it. Each repetition of a form that we perform in our taiji practice causes this flow to take place three extra times throughout the body.

In addition, each posture represents a particular combat tactic whose performance causes the qi to go from the lower *tantien* (a point about 3 inches below the navel) to the appropriate attacking portion of one's body. Because of the nature of these movements, the qi flows through the main organs in order to perform this work, and so from a war art we have a healing art.

This healing art is based upon the *wushu,* or war arts, because the fighting arts have always been an essential aspect of Chinese culture. I suppose if taijiquan had been invented in the United States, we would have movements derived from basketball or baseball to give us the appropriate flow of qi.

In this book I will not discuss the most dangerous area of taiji (i.e., *dim-mak,* or death-point striking), as I have covered it in detail in other books published by Paladin Press. It is enough to tell about the relationship that taiji has to dim-mak.

The originator of taiji was Chang San-feng, who was a famous acupuncturist and traditional Chinese doctor born around 1270 A.D. Chang was already well versed in the hard boxing styles indigenous to the Shaolin Monastery but was not satisfied with the skills he had developed.

Consequently, he and two other skilled acupuncturists experimented on unwilling subjects obtained from the local jail to discover the most effective martial usages of the acupuncture points! They incorporated all of the strikes that caused great damage or death into their training methods. Eventually, Chang had what he knew to be the most deadly fighting system in China—one that required only medium force to immobilize or kill an attacker.

Chang, being quite concerned that others would steal his knowledge, devised a series of movements that would conceal his methods from casual observers and that he could teach his personal students without their killing people. This form eventually became known as taijiquan. Nowadays, not many people know about the deadly part of taiji, and those who do usually do not teach it, except to a favored few.

For those who wish to take taijiquan on to its secondary level as a self-defense art (and a damned good one), even without dim-mak there are other training methods and forms, faster and more explosive, that teach us this aspect.

However, the slow-moving taijiquan form *does* give us the three main prerequisites for any fighting art: perfect balance, coordination, and, above all, timing. Once you have gained these prerequisites, you are able to go on to the more advanced techniques in the pauchui (cannon fist) form, push-hands, da-lu, sansau, and long har quan (dragon prawn boxing).

In the first four chapters in this book I discuss qi and qigong; present the long, slow form from the Yang style of taijiquan at a basic level; discuss more advanced aspects of form practice; and describe the essential two-person exercise of tui-sau (push-hands) as well as related basic martial exercises. In the last chapter, Michael Babin demonstrates martial applications of some of the major postures from the long form and discusses self-defense. It is my sincere wish that the following pages will help you gain some insights into your own martial training.

—ERLE MONTAIGUE

*   *   *   *   *

I have had many instructors since I began studying the Yang style in the mid-70s, and with hindsight I can safely say that I have learned something—either good or bad—from each of them.

My present teacher and friend, Master Erle Montaigue, has inspired me for the past three years with his skill, knowledge, and enthusiasm, and I am very proud to have assisted him in the creation of this book. It is an indication of his character that he insisted that we share the byline; not many instructors would have been as honest or as generous!

To his further credit, Erle encourages his senior students to become their own masters and not to look to him for all the answers. Consequently, some of the methods and opinions that appear in the chapter I wrote are the result of my own experience and research. So if you disagree with my statements, lay the blame at my feet, not his.

As is often the case, appearances are deceiving, and taijiquan is more demanding physically and mentally than is first apparent to the casual observer.

Initially, you learn a sequence of postures performed slowly in an exercise called "doing form," great attention being placed on the role of the mind, deep breathing, and proper body mechanics. With time, effort, and proper instruction, you supplement such practice with a variety of solo and interactive exercises. This improves the technical expression of your form so as to improve the quality and quantity of your qi and create both good health and martial skills that could be used for self-defense.

Unfortunately, it is not enough to simply practice form to achieve this. Competent instruction and a hunger for understanding are essential if you are to continue to refine and learn from your practice as opposed to just going through the motions—even if you are going through those motions on a technically skillful level.

Complacency is the great enemy of long-term progress. It afflicts instructors as well as beginners and is very difficult to overcome. At its extreme, it is characterized by those instructors who know barely more than their students and are content to remain at that level, year after year, even though they are aware of their low level of competence.

The opposite of complacency is the need to understand, and, at its best, it is characterized by the ongoing need to discover and digest those aspects of taiji that make it different from any other martial art or mind/body discipline. At its worst, this need can degenerate into a dissatisfaction with one's efforts that is expressed through constant changes of style or instructors.

While it is possible to gain some benefit, both physical and emotional, from even the most mediocre practice of taiji, it remains true in this art, as in life, that you get the most benefit from training correctly.

Instructors of Erle's caliber are rare, but they do exist and can be sought out; however, the best instruction in the world is no substitute for your own effort and patience. Fortunately, the art is such that you can practice and refine your understanding of that practice even into old age.

It took almost 17 years before my expression of taiji became in any way internal, but don't be discouraged by that. You may well have more aptitude or work harder than I did for the first few years!

In the end, the knowledge, forms, and methods outlined in this book are useless to you and your potential understanding of taiji if they stay on your shelf collecting dust. You need to expend a great deal of effort to become "effortless."

If you train moderately and regularly, you can enjoy and benefit from taijiquan until the day you die. I hope that this book will help you enjoy and improve your training in some small way.

—MICHAEL BABIN

chapter one

The word *qigong* (*ch'i kung* in those texts using the old Wade-Giles system of translating Chinese into English) literally means "internal work." In fact, any physical and/or mental actions combined with certain breathing methods that cause an internal flow of energy can be considered qigong. In physical terms, such "work" can be done while reclining, sitting, standing, or moving in a prescribed manner.

Taijiquan form is a type of moving qigong and, when done correctly, is an excellent means of improving health and martial skill. However, initially, even with competent instruction and effort, it is difficult to train internally because there are many physical aspects and technical details to coordinate: remembering the postures and sequence, proper breathing, yin-yang in the wrists and feet, and so on.

Standing qigong eliminates many of these physical details, making it easier to concentrate on breathing and developing *sung,* which is usually (though not quite accurately) translated as relaxation. Chang Yiu-chun, my main instructor in recent years, compared sung to baking a cake. You take the cake out of the oven and it has a nice high top on it. You turn away for a moment and in that time it has dropped even though you have not seen it drop. This is what sung is—moving without feeling the

QIGONG
THEORY
AND
PRACTICE

1

movement. For example, you are on the way to understanding sung when, while performing the group of postures known as Cloud Hands, you feel no tension or changes of state from yin to yang (or vice-versa) in the wrists while doing the movements.

Since standing is not as comfortable as sitting, you must concentrate on the principles of relaxation and body balance to do such exercise—even on a physical level. As in taiji, the entire body must learn to use only the appropriate muscles to do the "job" at hand—not too much effort, not too little.

The upper body in particular must be relaxed, and, although it's difficult, the mind must be encouraged to give up its obsession with endless mental "chatter." Paying attention to the breath is one method of slowing down and eventually stopping mental restlessness.

There are hundreds of different types of qigong, including those postures from the taiji forms, etc. But don't be alarmed and think that you will have to spend your whole life learning if you wish to pursue this activity!

There are so many variations because the experts in the different provinces of China each slightly modified what they learned to make the exercise their own while still attaining the same effect. Most provinces have their own "folk qigongs," and, not surprisingly, each claims that its is the best.

There are even qigong tournaments held in China each year in which practitioners compete to see how many bricks, supported on their bare heads, can be crushed by sledgehammers. However, we are not concerned with such theatrical displays.

Qigong has become a fashionable therapy in the West in the past decade and continues to gain popularity in much the same way that taijiquan did in the 70s and 80s. This ancient healing art is, in fact, ideal for people of all ages, affecting not only physical health but also psychological states.

QI THEORY

Within the body, there are 12 main and eight extra acupuncture meridians or channels. It is said that a bioelectrical force called qi flows freely through these channels to all of our internal organs.

Qi is to us as water is to the fish in the sea. They don't know it's there until they are taken out of it and they soon die. It's the same with us: block the flow of energy and we soon become sick and die.

We are told through ancient Chinese texts that whatever the external body does, so too does the internal flow of qi try to emulate. So it stands to reason that if we are performing harsh, unnatural movements that go against the natural bodily flow, so too will the internal flow of qi be impeded.

However, if we perform natural, flowing movements, we can enhance the natural internal flow of qi to all parts of the body. The many variations of stationary or standing qigong are designed to build up our prenatal qi, while it is the job of the taijiquan form, as a type of moving qigong, to cause this extra energy to flow freely to all parts of the body.

Taijiquan is a way to bring our energy flow back to normal and open the meridians so that the flow will be unimpeded. Taijiquan is closely related to acupuncture. Acupuncture is said to cure the immediate aliment, while taijiquan heals the root cause and stops it from returning. Every posture from taijiquan sends the qi to the organ associated with a particular acupuncture meridian. Some of the movements are repeated because these belong to the most important organs.

With time and progress, qi and blood circulation improve, helping lower high blood pressure and move qi down to the lower abdomen. Breathing becomes naturally slower and its rhythm more even without your having forced it to do so.

Can Qigong Be Harmful?

If you only practice the basic qigong stances and movements without overdoing them, there can be no danger. At the very worst, you will only be wasting your time and effort if you practice incorrectly. You cannot create a diseased state by not doing the exercises perfectly.

However, as in anything, if you practice qigong to excess,

there can be a harmful effect. This is where your teacher must guide you through the basics and slowly up to the advanced forms. For instance, if you are told not to attempt a certain qigong stance because it is an advanced practice, then you simply must not practice it prematurely. Many students are eager to learn or impatient, so they try to practice certain qigong stances long before they are ready, which leaves them open to a certain amount of harm. The danger lies in the fact that once we have established a certain flow by practicing a certain method, we are sometimes fooled into believing that we are able to take much more than our bodies are physically capable of at that time.

When this happens we are literally held in place by the flow of qi, our muscles having given up long ago. If that flow is suddenly interrupted, perhaps by a telephone call, the conscious mind takes over again. The great flow of energy slows to the normal rate, and we go back to using our physical muscles again. But our muscles are useless because they have been overused, and we collapse. I experienced this phenomenon during my initial training, and it has since happened to three of my students. Why? Because we all did something that our teachers told us not to. (But then what inquiring mind can resist doing something that someone warns against because it is too powerful!) This is the only drawback I have ever found in the practice of qigong for the average person.

However, if a person has certain serious ailments, such as blood clots, kidney stones, etc., there is some risk. The qigong tries to release these blockages, and this can cause great pain and sometimes immobility. Similarly, if a person has some mental disorder, it is inadvisable to do even the basic qigong for any length of time without having an instructor on hand, as qigong can cause the mentally ill to be more so.

The Main Categories of Qigong

All of the qigong techniques can be split up into three main categories: those for medical use, those for self-healing, and those for the martial arts. Usually, the self-healing and the martial arts aspects are of most interest to those who practice taijiquan.

By studying the self-healing qigongs, we can learn to use our own bodies and minds to heal ourselves of disease. When taijiquan is performed correctly and uses the four main breathing techniques (covered later), it also becomes a potent self-healing qigong practice.

When we practice the martial arts qigong, we make use of this internal work to gain power, speed, and timing for basic self-defense. At more advanced levels, we learn to "add" qi to an opponent's vital points to augment the damage caused by our physical strikes.

The more difficult "medical" qigong is used by a doctor of qigong to heal others. This very advanced practice not only involves the patient's learning and practicing self-healing qigong but also the doctor's intervention to either add or remove qi to aid the healing process. I am told that many traditional doctors in China are having a high success rate with cancer and other deadly diseases.

Taijiquan and Medical Qigong

A qigong healer is able to use the qigong stances to not only heal but also to diagnose any problems. First, on a large scale, the healer identifies the affected area of the body and determines whether the disease is "yin deficient" or "yang deficient."

On a very basic level, the healer accomplishes this by taking note of the position of the patient's palms after some minutes of the patient's having practiced his or her own qigong stance. (The positions of all of the limbs is also taken into account, as is the position of the fingers, but in this book I will only deal with the more simple palm positions.) If, for instance, the right palm has dropped to a lower level than the left palm, this indicates that there is a yang deficiency in the right side of the body. One has also to take into account the position of the other limbs to establish whether the upper or lower body is affected.

To further pinpoint the problem, the healer has the patient assume a variety of other postures, including some from the taijiquan form, to find out which ones cause pain or are comparatively more difficult than the others. If, for instance, the posture of

Brush Knee, Twist Step causes pain around the chest area and is more difficult than normal for a beginner to perform, this would indicate a yang-deficient heart problem. Further analysis of tongue, face, and skin condition would confirm the diagnosis.

The qigong doctor then has to decide how to heal the ailment. He may use acupuncture to heal the immediate effect of the pain and then use some qigong postures to put some yang energy into the heart. He may also practice his own qigong before treating the patient. For a minor ailment this might be for 20 minutes. For a more serious ailment he may practice qigong for a much longer period and fast, except for fruit, over a number of days.

He will then place his palms around the affected area or over the relevant acupuncture point and direct his own yang energy into these points to further the cure. His or her energy is released from a point on the palms called Laogung (Pericardium 8). If you close your fist and see where the longest finger points to, this is the point to which I am referring.

The doctor may also prescribe certain qigongs to cure the disease. This will sometimes be a taiji posture, usually the same one that was used to diagnose the disease. It may be a static posture used with certain breathing techniques—either a cleansing breath (inhaling through the nose and exhaling through the mouth) or a tonic breath (inhaling through the mouth and exhaling through the nose), using a prenatal or postnatal reverse of natural breathing (covered later in this book) or it may be a moving posture. For instance, to heal an ailment involving the joints, Single Whip may be used as a static posture. This same posture is used to heal the digestive tract, the only difference being that it is preceded by the posture of Press Forward, as in the taijiquan form, and is held for a few minutes, then repeated.

PRACTICING BASIC QIGONG FOR OVERALL GOOD HEALTH

Stand straight with your shoulders relaxed and gently round-ed, neither hunched forward nor held stiffly. The feet should be a little more than shoulder-width apart and parallel to each other. The arms should be hanging at both sides with fingers relaxed. Lift the arms in front with the palms facing each other, making sure not to lift or tense the shoulders.

Slowly draw the palms in toward the chest and start to bend your knees. The elbows should be bent no more than 90 degrees. You should feel as though you are holding a large ball in front of your torso (fig. 1).

The knees should bend only to the point where there is a vertical line between the second toe and the knee cap.

Figure 1

The back should be straight with the buttocks tucked under as if you were sitting on the edge of a high chair. This is the natural position for the lower back when the knees are partially bent. There should be no sway in the lower back.

You can do no harm to your back or any other part of your body as long as you are doing the stance correctly, with the spine straight and vertical to the ground, with no sway in the lower-back or lumbar region. After all, the backbone is being held in its natural position when your legs are bent. Our backbones naturally have a slight S shape. One person I know of teaches qigong with the buttocks sticking out while the legs are bent. This will cause both physical pain and energy blockages.

If you do feel pain, check your posture. If it is correct, then the pain is probably because your backbone is out of alignment and the qigong is trying to heal the problem. In such a case, only perform qigong for short periods until the pain goes away. The chin should be pulled in slightly but not so much as to pull the head down. This tends to straighten the backbone. Your eyes should be looking straight ahead, but not staring. They can be half-closed but not shut.

Press the tongue lightly upward against the hard palate behind the front teeth, as if saying the letter L, in order to join the yin and yang acupuncture meridians so that the qi can flow freely in the upper heavenly circulation. This occurs via a most important pathway, which begins at a point called the Conceptor Vessel 1 (Cv 1), situated next to the anus. The flow through this path, which is called the Governor's Vessel and is yang, continues up the backbone with the inhalation, over the skull, down the front of the forehead, and into the top of the hard palate. The qi then continues down via the tongue to meet with the yin Conceptor Vessel at the base of the tongue, where it continues down the front of the body to the tan-tien. With each inhalation, the qi travels up the yang meridian, and with each exhalation, it travels down the yin meridian.

You must breathe like a child. As you inhale, the area just below your chest must expand. If you are totally relaxed, especially the shoulders and chest area, then this is the only way that you can breathe. Just allow your stomach to stick out when you inhale. As you exhale, the area that has filled up with air must obviously contract, and so the stomach area goes in.

Many people have difficulty with this. It is tension that causes us to lift the chest when we breathe. The qi rises up into your chest, and you become tense and top-heavy. Breathe slowly but naturally and only as your own rhythm dictates. Don't force your breath; only inhale until it stops naturally and then wait until you want to exhale naturally. There should be a slight pause between the in and out breaths.

The fingers should be held lightly apart and turned out slightly. There should be a straight line of skin between the thumb and forefinger, as shown in Figure 2.

This activates an important acupuncture point called Colon 4 (Co 4), just where the thumb and forefinger meet at the back of the hand. (Applying firm pressure to this point is

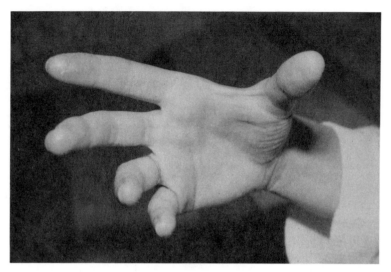

Figure 2

very good for healing headaches in the front of the head.
However, don't stimulate it during pregnancy, as it can cause
contractions in the womb.) Holding the palms this way causes
the thumb to become "yang" while the fingers become "yin."
This is said to "bring the large circle into the palm" (causing a
concentration of energy in the whole body) and is most important for developing both healing and, in particular, martial
skills, as it concentrates the energy in the palms.

The toes should be held slightly concave so that another
important point on the bottom of the foot is activated. This
point, called Kidney 1 (K1), is called the "Bubbling Well,"
from which the qi is said to spring. (For the configuration of
the foot and the location of Kidney 1 point, see figs. 3 and
4.) The qi must be brought from the lower tan-tien down to
this point in order to be used. Holding the foot so that it is
slightly concave causes Kidney 1 to become yin, while the
outside of the foot becomes yang, which attracts yang energy
down to the point so that we can utilize it in the martial arts
or for healing.

The elbows should be held as if you have a tennis ball under each arm. This is good for the flow of qi and allows the shoulders

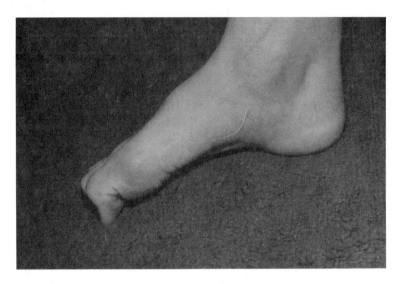

Figure 3

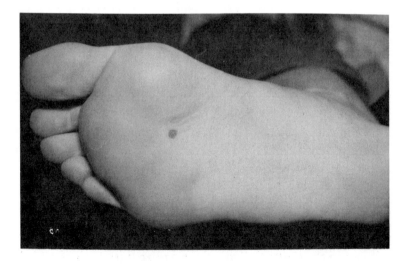

Figure 4

to relax more. The stomach should be held totally relaxed and the anal sphincter held lightly closed.

Try to "sit" into the posture and feel the perfect balance that it brings. Do not lean in any direction. A full-length mirror can be useful for checking this. The Taoist basis of qigong suggests muscle energy is a necessary catalyst for the process of converting qi to jing. In standing qigong, this is brought about by bending the knees, which creates energy/heat in the lower tan-tien. This, in turn, brings about the chemical changes in the body that are needed for the conversion. It's like lighting a fire under a cauldron to heat the water in it. The resulting steam, a purified, condensed form of water, rises and can be used as an energy source.

Quite often you will experience the "shakes" or trembling in various part of the body when doing standing qigong. This is because the qi flows down to the Bubbling Well easily but encounters tension caused by some blockage on the way back. As the obstruction clears, the shakes will go and you will be able to feel things. (I am purposely vague in saying "things," because if I tell you what to expect then you will look for that particular feeling. One of my main teachers told me that qi is like a very shy person; if you stare at it, it will leave and won't be seen again for some time. The best way to experience something is not to expect anything in particular, just let it come!) Be aware of your legs—sometimes they slowly creep upward and the knees straighten without your even knowing it. This is the case when people say that they do not experience any vibration or shakes.

For the first few times that you are standing in this position and trying to follow all of these directions, you may wonder, "Why am I doing this?" Persevere and you will discover the great benefits of this practice. If you feel tension, just breathe it away with each exhalation.

As you stand in this or any qigong postures, think of beautiful things and imagine that a string is holding you up from the crown of your head. Have a slight smile on your face and "think under" (i.e., think about the underside of your arms or legs).

Figure 5

Figure 6

This will cause your limbs to feel heavy and cause the subconscious mind to focus on the lower tan-tien.

End your qigong session by dropping your arms slowly until they are roughly in line with your navel with the palms up, as shown in Figure 5.

Hold this posture for about one-third of the total time of each qigong session. Finally, as you inhale, bring both arms up and out to your sides with relaxed wrists (fig. 6).

Then, as shown in Figure 7, the arms continue across in front of the chest and push downward to the sides as you exhale and straighten your legs.

Do not make any sudden movements or have anything cold to drink for at least five minutes. Just walk around slowly.

There are four hand positions that can be used to cause different energy activations to take place when doing this basic qigong. For instance, holding the palms as was just described, in what is called the "mother" position, sends 60 percent of activated qi to the legs, with the rest going to the hands. This is the position normally used for overall self-healing.

If the palms are facing away from you with the thumbs pointing downward, called the "father" position, more qi is activated in the legs, and one builds strength, particularly in the upper body.

If the palms are facing downward (without changing the relative position of the arms and body), called the "daughter" position, more qi is activated in the arms and hands. This is good for any forearm or hand ailments such as RSI (repetitive strain injury).

When the palms are held facing each other with the thumbs pointing upward, called

Figure 7

the "son" position, more qi is activated in the spine as well as the lungs and internal organs, so it is good for breathing ailments, etc.

ADVANCED STANDING QIGONG

There is a more advanced form of qigong in which the weight is placed fully onto one leg. You should not attempt this until you can hold the basic qigong for at least 20 minutes.

As shown in Figure 8, the arms are held as if holding a baby (front palm cradling the head, rear palm holding the bum), and one foot is placed, empty of weight, in front of the other. All other aspects are the same as for the basic qigong.

You must recognize the following three signs while performing this more advanced qigong:

1) You will feel as if you just can't stand there for another second, and this can happen after only about one

Figure 8

minute. You must rec-
ognize a pain in the
standing leg as if a hot
needle is being stuck
into your thigh.

2) If you are able to
stand this for a little
longer, you will feel
this heat dissipate,
bringing relief and a
warm feeling that rolls
over your thigh.

3) Your leg will shake,
and when this happens
you should change
legs and do the pos-
ture on the other side.

You will notice that you are now able to stand for a little
longer on the other side; this is because the qi has begun to flow.
When you switch back to the first leg you will again find that you
are able to stand for a longer period, and so on.

At first you should try standing this way for only about one
and a half minutes on each leg; this will be enough. As the qi is
built up in the legs, you will be able to increase this time. But you
must look for the three signs, which will be your best indication
as to how long to stand on each leg.

BREATHING TECHNIQUES FOR QIGONG

There are four main breathing techniques that should be
used with qigong: 1) natural breath, which was described previously; 2) reverse breath, in which the abdomen is sucked in
with each inhalation and relaxed with the subsequent exhala-

tion; 3) prenatal breath, in which a rolling action of the abdomen occurs (the lower abdomen is sucked in with the inhalation while the upper abdomen is pushed out, then the lower abdomen is pushed out on the exhalation while the upper abdomen is sucked in); and 4) tortoise breath, an advanced prenatal breath in which we hold the inhalation for seven seconds. Tortoise breath gives the two energies—inner and outer—a chance to mix at the "border" (the diaphragm). When we exhale, the inner qi (below the diaphragm) takes a little of the outer qi (the inhaled air) with it to the lower tantien, thus increasing our store of internal energy.

THE TAIJI POSTURES FOR SELF-HEALING

Taijiquan wasn't worked out in a haphazard way by successive generations of masters who hoped that these exercises would work upon the internal organs somehow to give the practitioner great health. Rather, each posture was created deliberately to stretch the correct muscle groups and tendons and act upon the acupuncture meridians associated with that area in accordance with the theories of Chinese traditional medicine (CTM).

The Japanese healing massage method called *shiatsu* uses the same principles and activates the points with finger pressure to beneficially affect the acupuncture points. Shiatsu, of course, came from the Chinese healing science of acupuncture, to which taijiquan is related and concomitant.

According to CTM, the quality and quantity of internal energy flowing through the meridians constantly waxes and wanes as influenced by a variety of factors, including our fitness levels, the weather, emotion, diet, and environment (i.e., pollution). When qi is distributed evenly and at the optimum levels, we are healthy and able to resist disease.

Taiji, as a potent form of moving qigong, uses the various postures in the form to send this bioelectrical energy to various parts of the body. Taiji form is mainly used as an excellent method of preventative medicine; each posture is said to activate one of the 12 meridians, thus giving the whole body an internal *and* external workout. In addition, however, these postures can be used as static or moving qigong. Each individual posture can also be used as a static posture in a qigong stance to heal the associated organ. Sometimes we have to take a couple of the movements on either side of a posture, moving in and out of the posture to heal certain organs. Interestingly, this same posture, when used as a static qigong, may heal a completely different organ.

NOTE: Treating specific ailments in an acute or severe chronic state is best accomplished in conjunction with a qualified expert.

It is important to remember that the seriously ill in China are treated by experts who usually combine qigong with traditional healing methods (i.e., massage, herbal medicine, acupuncture) or Western medicine to benefit the patient. A patient may do *hours* of moving and/or static qigong each day for many weeks as part of his or her treatment. Such practice is carefully monitored. Self-diagnosis and treatment by amateurs is usually foolish and may be fatal in the case of life-threatening illness. Using the wrong posture for your particular health needs won't aggravate the existing condition or create new ones; however, you will have wasted your time and effort in terms of healing the main condition, which, if it is acute, could have serious ramifications.

When doing a posture that requires you to hold the end of it as a standing meditation, remember to do it on both sides of the body (i.e., mirror image). This is particularly important when you do several repetitions so you avoid overstraining the muscles of one leg. Aside from the mechanical stress this causes, it is important to remember that muscle tension is said to block qi flow.

Below is the complete list of organs healed by the different postures. These have been worked out scientifically over the generations by the various taijiquan masters who were, for the most part, also doctors of Chinese traditional medicine. I have also worked with prominent acupuncturists and shiatsu experts to verify these postures and the meridians upon which they work.

ORGAN	POSTURES	STATE	CONDITION
COLON	Use Grasp Bird'sTail up to Push. Repeat 10 times.	Yang	For a yin disease such as diarrhea, use this qigong only.
	Use the qigong for the lungs, i.e., Fishes in Eight. Go into it 10 times and hold as qigong for one minute.	Yin	Use this as well as the above if the state is yang, such as constipation.
LUNGS	Fishes in Eight.	Yang	Use by itself if a yang condition, like inflammation, etc. But OK for all lung ailments.
	Grasp Bird's Tail as above.	Yang	Use if fluid in the lungs, etc., along w/Fishes in Eight or as an adjunct to it.
SPLEEN	High Pat on Horse. Use as static qigong, holding five minutes on each side. Or use Horse's Mane as moving qigong.	Yin	Use if too much yang in spleen.
LUNGS/ COLON	Pulling the Bow, plus Lift Hands to Heaven (that whole section that involves those two). Repeat five times.	—	Use if overall toning needed in both these areas.
LUNGS/ SPLEEN	In general, use Stroking the Horse's Mane. Be sure to swivel on heels. Repeat five times, holding for three minutes.	—	Use when spleen or lungs are malfunctioning. A general toner for these organs.

ORGAN	POSTURES	STATE	CONDITION
STOMACH	Tan Pien (Single Whip). Use as static qigong to aid digestion. Or Wave Hands Like Clouds to balance out the energy.	Yang	Use Tan Pien for all stomach ailments or if too little stomach activity, i.e., too yin. Use Wave Hands to balance chi.
	Golden Cock Stands on One Leg. Use as static qigong for three minutes on each leg.	—	Overall stomach problems.
	Hold Brush Knee Twist Step (BKTS) as static qigong on each side for five minutes. Repeat three times.	—	Same as above.
	Play Guitar. Go into this from BKTS. Hold five minutes and repeat five times.	—	Aids in digestion.
	Wave Hands Like Clouds.	Yang	Use if not enough stomach activity. Good qigong for stomach overall.
	Horse's Mane, use w/Wave Hands.	Yin	Use if too yang in stomach.
	Perform from Push to Apparent Close-Up and hold at end for one minute. Repeat 10 times.	—	Use for general gastric troubles.
	Wave Hands Like Clouds. Generally repeat 10 x 4 steps, but do as many as you like.	—	Same as above.
SPLEEN	Wave Hands Like Clouds.	Yin	Use w/the main one of Tan Pien if stomach activity too yang, i.e., heartburn, etc.

ORGAN	POSTURES	STATE	CONDITION
SPLEEN/STOMACH	Wave Hands Like Clouds.	Yang	Use w/the above if too little spleen activity, i.e., too yin.
LIVER	Step Back and Repulse Monkey.	Yang	Use w/the above if a yin condition exists, e.g., dull and listless, etc.
GALL BLADDER/LIVER	Step Back and Repulse Monkey, Yang Cheng-fu.	Yang	If too yin, not enough bile, etc., or gall bladder is not working well. If bad lower back pain, especially in mornings, repeat five times, but also use for overall gall bladder.
	Lift Hands from Flying into It and hold for five minutes. on both sides.	Yin	Use if too much bile or activity too yang. Use w/the above.
	Lift Hands as static qigong.	Yin	Use by itself for all liver ailments, but in particular if too angry (red face, etc.), i.e., too yang.
HEART	Brush Knee Twist Step. Moving qigong.	Yin	Use for all heart states, but in particular if too much fire in heart, can't sleep, etc. Also for pre-ejaculation.
SMALL INTESTINE	Fan through Back. Hold the static qigong for five minutes.	Yang	Use by itself for general small intestine conditions, but in particular if too little activity in small intestine, i.e., too yin.
SMALL INTESTINE/HEART	Fan through Back	Yang	Use if too much sleep, not enough sexual urge, etc.

ORGAN	POSTURES	STATE	CONDITION
SMALL INTESTINE/ HEART	Brush Knee Twist Step.	Yin	Use w/Fan through back if too much small intestine activity, i.e., too yang.
KIDNEYS	Spin Around and Kick, Yang Cheng-fu style.	Yin	Use if too fearful.
	Snake Creeps Down. Repeat and hold three times on each side for three minutes if possible, less if not.	—	Use if kidneys need toning in general.
BLADDER	Mailed Fist and tan-tien pushing, from old Yang, plus bit from end when fist comes over face and around, bending backwards, etc.	Yang	Use for great sorrow.
	Spin around and Kick. Use w/the above.	Yin	Unbalanced emotions.
KIDNEYS/ BLADDER	(Use w/the above.) Mailed Fist, old Yang, as well as tan-tien pushing and bit from end as above.	Yang	Use if too fearful.
TRIPLE WARMER	In general, start w/Three Warmer qigong exercise.	—	This organ, generally not known about in Western medicine, is used for irreg-ularity in other organs and if amount of yin and yang energy is unbalanced.
GATE OF LIFE ORGAN	Use the Opening of the Gates for this one.	—	Use for too little semen production in males and menstrual problems in females. Use if regenerative energy is irregular or if person is depressed. Again, this organ is generally unknown in the West.

ORGAN/AREA	POSTURES	STATE	CONDITION
ALL OF THE INTERNAL ORGANS	Go into Embrace Tiger, Return to Mountains from Cross Hands. Repeat 10 times.	—	Use if organs are in need of rejuvenation in general.
CNS	Shoulder Press. Go into it from Pull Back and hold for five minutes, then go into Stork Spreads Wings and hold for five minutes.	—	Acts upon the cerebrum, making it more alert. Good for exams, etc.
SPINAL COLUMN	Use Lift Hands as moving and static qigong.	—	Use to make spinal column more elastic. Also for dry or wrinkled skin, to maintain more youthful appearance.
GLANDS	Step Forward, Parry, and Punch, from BKTS to punch. Hold at end for three minutes, repeat five times.	—	Use if glands are not functionng optimally.
JOINTS	Move into Tan Pien from Fishes in Eight and hold for three minutes on each leg.	—	Use for joint ailments.
BLOOD CIRC.	General Step Forward to Seven Stars. Hold as static qxigong for three minutes on each leg. Repeat three times.	—	Use for bad circulation.

ORGAN/AREA	POSTURES	STATE	CONDITION
—	From old Yang style use Fist under Elbow as many times as you like. Also use Lotus Kick.	—	Use if overweight.
—	Turn around and Chop with Fist, Yang Cheng-fu style.	—	Use if overweight.
—	Use Fist under Elbow from Yang Cheng-fu form and hold as qigong for five minutes each side.	—	Use if underweight.
—	Needle at Sea Bottom. Go into this one from BKTS, hold for one minute, then slowly come up and repeat on other side.	—	Use to increase the life force to the spine, especially when used w/Lotus Kick, Yang Chen-fu style.
—	Separation of Right and Left Foot, Yang Cheng-fu style.	Yin	Use if person is too yang, angry, red in face, etc.
—	Separation of Left and Right Foot, old Yang style.	Yang	Use if person is too yin, too laid back. Lack of energy.
—	Sitting Like a Duck posture. Go into it from standing if possible. Hold for three minutes on each side. Not good for older people who are arthritic, etc.	—	Body in need of rejuvenation.

YIN ORGANS	YANG ORGANS	IMPLICATIONS
These yin organs store energy for later use:	These yang organs activate energy, i.e., cause storage organs to release it to perform some function:	An imbalance of yin or yang energy in these main organs causes disease, so we try to balance the yin and yang energy using the above postures as qigongs.
Liver	Gall Bladder	
Heart	Small Intestine	
Spleen	Stomach	
Lungs	Large Intestine/Colon	
Kidneys	Bladder	

chapter two

Learning taiji form is a complex task for many modern people because they have lost the ability to learn new skills involving both physical and mental activity. Regaining the ability to learn is largely a matter of self-discipline, brought about by the desire to experience the lessons that taiji can teach. This can be encouraged in the following ways:

1) Create a written training schedule and set some goals. Keep a daily training diary, even for those days that you don't train. (Studying the reasons that you didn't practice on any given day may help you identify behavioral patterns that are counterproductive to your training).

2) Expect setbacks. Accept the inevitable missed classes and minor aches and pains or injuries as delays, not as signs that you should give up your practice.

3) Give yourself credit when it's appropriate. Executing a difficult physical move or having a sudden insight into some aspect of your training should be acknowledged with pride. Just remember to keep "self-congratulation" in perspective. It is also important to remember

TAIJI

LONG

FORM

that progress in any aspect of learning taiji usually occurs as part of a cumulative—and challenging—process rather than a sudden breakthrough. While it is true that a minority of gifted students seem to have one intuitive breakthrough after another in their training, most of us will plod along, creating an internal understanding of ourselves and our martial art one piece at a time.

The following long, slow form comes to us from Yang Ch'eng-fu, the last grandmaster of the Yang style, through his eldest son, the late Yang Sau-chung, who taught in Hong Kong until his death in May 1985. Ch'eng-fu continued to modify his form during his teaching career, and there were at least three "official" versions. Sau-chung learned and continued to teach his father's original modification of the old Yang style, dating back to the early 1920s.

GENERAL RULES FOR PRACTICE

- The head should not turn independently of the torso— let your eyes do the looking, keeping your nose centered over your navel. Even when you have to look, for instance, to the front while you turn your waist to the side, you should look out of the corners of your eyes rather than turning your head prematurely.

- The head should not bob up and down when you are taking steps. By keeping your knees bent, you should be able to avoid this. Be sure that you have the majority of your weight on one leg before you move or pivot the other.

- Never let the knees extend past the tips of the toes. (Be aware of the fact that when you look down at your toes, there is a slight parallax visual error that distorts your perception.)

- Start out with a high posture: the knees bend only a little and the steps are not too long. There are three levels of posture—high, medium, and low. The low level, in which the stance is long and the knees well-bent, should only be attempted after many years of practice, and only when you are able to do it without creating tension.

- Large stances should not involve extending the knees past the toes; the stance becomes longer to compensate for this. As you progress even further and the form becomes more internal than physical, the step will rise again, so that you perform the form at a more natural stance.

- The shoulders are rounded and the elbows dropped and relaxed. Keeping the elbows, in general, pointing downward encourages the shoulders to relax. However, this is one of the most difficult aspects of taiji for beginners to achieve.

- The fingers should be straight but not stiff. The palms are relaxed and slightly hollowed while holding the Tile Palm Hand.

- The backbone should be, in general, vertical in relation to the ground, but there are some postures that require a *slight* forward lean. Never hunch the back.

- Walk like a cat, stepping carefully and softly, so that if there were danger you would be able to take that foot back instantly. Land on the heel when stepping forward and on the ball of the foot when stepping to the rear.

- Avoid being "double-weighted" (i.e., having your weight equally distributed between both feet). Be aware of which leg is yang (weighted) and which is yin (non-weighted). Only at the very beginning and the end of the form should the weight be evenly distributed. There must, of course, be a time in each posture during which you are double-weighted as you shift from one leg to the other, but this should be only momentary.

- Never have equal strength in your palms, as this is also a variation of being double-weighted.

- Maintain a physical and psychological sense of equilibrium in relation to the earth (i.e., a sense of being "grounded"); never commit yourself fully—always have in mind the possibility of retreating if you advance or of advancing if you retreat.

- In lifting up or pulling back, inhale; in pushing forward or stepping downward, exhale.

- The classics say that the qi springs from the feet, is directed by the waist, and is manifested in the fingers. However, the qi really comes from the lower tan-tien.

- Your head should be held as if suspended from above by string. This will pull your backbone up and sink the qi to the lower tan-tien.

- Try not to stop at the end of each posture once you start feeling comfortable with them. The movements should flow together in a slow and even rhythm.

WHEN AND HOW TO TRAIN

I recommend that at each practice session you do the form three times: once for the bones, muscles, and sinews; once for the mind; and once for the spirit. The first time should be done in about 10 or 15 minutes, the second in about 20 to 30 minutes, and the last in about 40 minutes.

The classical times to practice were said to be as follows:

Dawn—when you are coming out of yin and entering yang.

Mid-day—when you are in extreme yang.

Dusk—when you are coming out of yang and entering yin.

Midnight—when you are in extreme yin.

In traditional terms, following this schedule would give you a completely balanced practice structure. However, most of us are doing very well if we practice at dawn and dusk.

The length and frequency of each of your training sessions depends on your level of interest, physical ability, time constraints, and the recommendations of your instructor. Few modern teachers, much less their students, practice with the intensity that the old masters brought to their training. Of course, in those days the latter had to be skilled at a variety of methods and weapons, because they never knew when they would be challenged by a rival. In addition, instructors had to be ready for challenges that frequently led to severe injury or death and *had* to train at a level of intensity that is alien to most of us.

These days, few of us with families or occupations can match such training regimens, but regular practice remains essential to making progress—especially if your interest goes beyond doing forms. It is difficult to be patient with those taiji practitioners and instructors who obviously believe that doing a form once a day somehow makes them superior to a young hard-stylist who practices one or two hours a day.

Interestingly, modern research has shown that the traditionalists were intuitively on track with regard to times of the day to practice. According to Dr. David W. Hill of the University of North Texas at Denton, as reported in *Redbook* (Sept. 1993), studies have shown that people are more inclined to skip scheduled exercise in the afternoon because of fatigue or busy schedules. However, high-intensity activity, (like fast or fast/slow forms) that require short bursts of energy are best done late in the day. You'll feel stronger, perform more skillfully, and get more out of your workout. For slower, steadier exercise (such as slow form), you'll reap the same benefits whether it's early or late in the day.

It should be self-evident to anyone whose feet are on the ground (in itself a prerequisite for the internal arts) that hard work and sweat must enter into your study of the effortless arts, especially for the first few years.

THE "ORIGINAL" YANG CH'ENG-FU FORM: PART ONE

For the purposes of footwork, refer to the direction that you are facing initially as north.

Preparation

Stand with your feet parallel and shoulder-width apart.

The palms are at your sides and slightly flexed, but not enough to create tension (fig. 9). This is called a "yang" palm (as opposed to a "yin" palm, which is totally relaxed). The elbows should be held slightly out from the body, as if you are holding a tennis ball under each arm. The energy is sunk to the lower tan-tien, partly as a result of your simply paying attention to that part of the body.

Raise Arms

Slowly and deliberately

Figure 9

raise your arms in front of you as if ropes are pulling both hands up and away from your body. There should be a slight forward rocking of the body to make the arms rise. The wrists relax as you inhale. The arms are as if you are sleep-walking (fig. 10), with the palms about six inches apart. Do not bend the elbows any more than they were before you began the movement.

Figure 10

As you exhale slowly, your body rocks slightly backward and the arms arc back down along their original path. The wrists change state gradually, returning to a flexed position. The wrists can be brought inward slightly, but do not make a large circle. Do not bend your knees at this point. Your palms end up where they started, as in Figure 9.

Push Left

Once again, slowly change the wrists to dropped (limp) position, and, as you inhale, bring both arms up and across your body to the northeast in an arc (fig. 11). The palms stay the same distance apart. Keep the left wrist at your center and away from your body.

Figure 11

Figure 12

Figure 13

Continue the circle back over to your northwest corner at about face height, and, as your left palm starts to come down, flex the wrist and exhale (fig. 12). The right wrist is relaxed and at your center. The left fingers are no higher than shoulder height, and the Co 4 points mentioned in Chapter 1 are in line.

Block to the Right

On that last exhalation, bring your left palm down and across your body to end up underneath your right palm (fig. 13). As you do this, bend the knees, placing 70 percent of your weight onto the left leg. Your right foot swivels on the heel so that the toes point to the northeast corner. Your eyes are still looking to the north, but the body has turned.

NOTE: Unless stated otherwise, your weight is always distributed 70 percent on one leg and 30 percent on the other.

P'eng

Shift your weight to your right leg as you inhale. Take a

step with your left foot to the north, touching down on the heel and maintaining a shoulder-width stance. Make sure that your stance doesn't end up too "skinny." Just extend your foot where it wants to go naturally but in line with its previous position. The foot should remain "weightless" until you consciously shift onto it.

As you turn your shoulders to the north, you bring 70 percent of your weight onto your left leg and exhale. The left arm comes up rounded in front of the solar plexus, and the right palm goes back down to your right side, as shown in Figure 14. You are now facing the north.

Figure 14

Block to the Left

Three movements happen simultaneously, as shown in Figure 15. Relax the right palm and bring it under the left. The left palm has turned down to meet it. Pick up the right heel and look to the east. Turn your torso to the northeast and inhale.

Double P'eng

Pick up your right foot

Figure 15

Figure 16

and place the heel down almost in the same spot but with the toes facing east. Shift your weight onto the right foot as the right palm comes up in front of your left palm, which does not move but only flexes. The two palms are as if you are holding a small ball on your centerline at about the height of your solar plexus (fig. 16).

You are now facing the east, and as you shifted forward you dragged your left toes around 45 degrees to face the northeast. Your weight is now on your right leg. Exhale.

Lu or Pull Back

Turn both palms over (pausing the breath) so that the right is down and the left is facing up. The fingers of the left hand should point into the thumb of the right hand (fig. 17). Pull both palms down to your left hip as your body turns to the northeast. Inhale. Your weight is all on the left leg.

Chee or Squeeze Forward

This posture is often mistranslated as Press. Place the heel of the left palm onto the

Figure 17

inside of the right wrist, which turns over to face you (fig. 18). Don't lift your palms up and then thrust them forward, but rather bring both palms up gradually as you shift forward to the east. Squeeze your elbow slightly inward and turn back to face the east as you finish the movement. Exhale.

Sit Back

Brush the top of your right hand with your left palm and extend your fingers with palms downward. As shown in Figure 19, sit back onto your left leg with your trunk slightly to your left and fold both palms in toward your body as you inhale. Keep the back vertical.

Figure 18

Press Forward

This posture is often mistranslated as Push. From the previous posture, lower your stance slightly, flex both palms, and exhale as you turn back to face the east and press your palms forward and upward while shifting onto your right leg (fig. 20).

NOTE: With any palm movement, imagine that you

Figure 19

Figure 20

Figure 21

are exhaling out of your palms from the lower tan-tien.

Sit Back, Ready

Shift the weight back onto your rear leg as you inhale. Drop the right wrist back to the same position held in Figure 19. As shown in Figure 21, drop the other arm to cross your chest with the fingers of your left hand pointing into your right elbow. You are still facing the east.

Fishes in Eight

With the weight on your left leg, swing both palms out to the northwest with the left palm leading and both palms flexed away from the movement as if the wind is blowing the fingers backward. As shown in Figure 22, swivel around 90 degrees on the heel of your right foot so that it faces north. The left foot is still facing northwest. As your left palm and body come around to point northwest, your right palm comes over to point into your left elbow. This is part of your exhalation.

The next half of this movement (fig. 23) uses the rest of that exhalation. Bring both palms in toward your chest, keeping the palms the same distance apart as you slowly start to change your weight. Turn your body into the northeast with the weight now on the right foot. The position of the feet has not changed.

This posture is the exact opposite of what is shown in Figure 22. You have now performed a counterclockwise lateral circle with both palms.

Single Whip

Make a counterclockwise hooking action with the right hand. As shown in Figure 24, all the fingers should be bent slightly, surrounding the thumb and pointing downward. The right arm straightens out and points to the northeast. (This is the only time a straight arm is used in taijiquan.) Your left palm turns in toward you, and the fingers almost touch the inside of your right elbow. Inhale.

Lift your left foot and, leaving the right arm where it is, turn your whole body around, taking your left arm with you in the same configuration as shown in Figure 24, the left wrist aligned with your

Figure 22

Figure 23

Figure 24

Figure 25

center. Place your left heel down to the west so that there is a shoulder-width distance between your heels laterally and the left foot is to the west as far as it will go without overreaching.

The breath has been held naturally. Just before the right heel touches the ground, you should lift your left elbow and do a small inward turning circle, pushing slightly to the west as your weight comes down onto the left leg (fig, 25). Your right toes are dragged around to point to the northwest by the turning of the waist once your body weight is firmly on the left leg. Exhale.

Lift Hands

Allow both palms to flex slightly as they are moved down about six inches as if the arms are wings. Now, on the inhalation, lift both palms up again about six inches and turn your left toes 45 degrees to point to the northwest (fig. 26). This is a weighted turn on the heel of the left foot.

NOTE: Whenever doing a weighted turn, it is essential to

turn the leg as a unit, with the movement being initiated in the hip socket, not the knee. Our hips are designed to rotate and should be used to initiate all weighted turns.

Flex both hands downward again and bring them down in two arcs to the front of your body. The left palm is pointing to your right elbow. Lift both palms up as if splashing water onto your face, still with the left palm near your right elbow. As the palms come up, you should lift up your right foot. This is all happening on the exhalation. As you lower your palms into position, your right heel touches the ground with no weight on it (fig. 27). The distance between the heels should be half of shoulder width.

Figure 26

Pull Down

From the last position, push both palms out slightly to the northwest as you shift a small amount of weight onto the right heel (about 10 percent). As shown in Figure 28, turn both palms over, right down and left up, and, as you inhale, pull down

Figure 27

Figure 28

Figure 29

to your left side as your body turns to the northwest.

Shoulder Press

From the last posture, take the left palm up in a circle and place it near your right triceps. As this happens, the right foot takes a small step to the northeast with the toes pointing to the north to make your stance shoulder width again. Your body is still turned to the northwest. Shift onto your right foot and attack with your shoulder as you exhale. Your right shoulder should be over your right knee and your back should be vertical, as shown in Figure 29. At this point your eyes are looking to the north but your head is in its correct position and faces the same direction as the body.

Stork Spreads Wings

Turn your body only slightly to the west as your right arm comes up with the wrist at your center, palm facing you (fig. 30). Your left palm comes down to your left side. The right palm comes up to chest height as part of your last exhalation.

As you inhale, continue the circle of the right palm until it comes over your head, and turn your body to the west. As shown in Figure 31, your left foot lifts up and is placed down in a "toe stance," with only the ball of the foot touching the floor (no weight is placed onto it). As you turn to the west and exhale, your right palm turns up, as if saluting.

Brush Knee, Twist Step (Left Foot Forward)

Drop your right palm down to your right hip, turning it to face upward as you do so. Don't allow your palm to go out to the side in a clockwise arc; just cascade it down. As this happens, the left palm relaxes and lifts above the right palm, as if both hands were holding a large ball (fig. 32). Inhale. Your body has turned to the northwest.

The left palm continues that same clockwise circle, downward and across the torso, and touches your left knee, which has lifted to meet it (fig. 33). As this happens, your right palm has lifted up and out to the height of the

Figure 30

Figure 31

Figure 32

Figure 33

right ear. The right palm should not make a large circle to the northeast but should start coming forward with the fingers relaxed. The breath at this point is held naturally, ready for the exhalation.

After you have brushed your left knee, your left heel steps to the southwest with the toes pointing to the west to initiate a forward bow stance. As the weight is rolled onto your left foot, the right palm should come to the west with the body and, at the last, should flex as the weight comes down onto the left foot (fig. 34). The rear toes are dragged around 45 degrees to face the northwest. The right index finger is in line with the nose. Exhale.

NOTE: This is a strike, not a pushing action. A push starts out with the palm already flexed, while the strike uses a flicking, driving movement of the wrist.

Play Guitar
Bending the knee, lift your right foot off the ground about six inches and

place it exactly where it was. Some teachers prefer to bring the foot forward at this point, but this is not correct, because the martial value of the "false step" is lost. The purpose of lifting the foot is to cause the left leg to become totally yang for maximum backward thrust.

As shown in Figure 35, lift the palms as you inhale and drop them into position as you exhale, bringing the left heel across slightly to form a "heel stance." This posture is the mirror image of Lift Hands (figs. 26 and 27), but the two postures have different applications.

Figure 34

Brush Knee, Twist Step (Left Foot Forward)

From the preceding posture, we now repeat exactly what we did after the Stork Spreads Wings posture (fig. 32): drop the right palm and bring the left palm over to your right corner to hold the ball as you inhale. Now repeat Brush Knee, Twist Step exactly as you did it previously (figs. 33 and 34). The only difference is that you do not have to drag the right toe around

Figure 35

Figure 36

Figure 37

because it was placed down facing the northwest.

Brush Knee, Twist Step (Right Foot Forward)

This is the mirror-image of what you just did. Do a weighted turn of the left leg so that the left toes point 45 degrees to the southwest. Remember to initiate the turn in the hip socket, not the knee. As shown in Figure 36, hold the ball to your left corner, right palm on the top as you inhale.

As you step to the west with your right foot, the right palm comes down and brushes the right knee as your left palm comes up to your left ear. Place the right foot down to the west and, as you roll onto it, strike with your left palm as before and exhale (fig. 37).

Brush Knee, Twist Step (Left Foot Forward)

Turn your right toes to the northwest, weighted on your heel, and hold the ball as you inhale (fig. 38).

Now, as in Figure 34, brush the left knee as it steps to the west and attack with your right palm.

Play Guitar
Repeat the movements depicted in Figure 35.

Brush Knee, Twist Step (Left Foot Forward)
Repeat the movements that followed Play Guitar, as in Figure 34.

NOTE: You have performed one Brush Knee, Twist Step followed by Play Guitar and then three Brush Knee, Twist Steps in a row (the first of which attacks with the right palm, the second with the left, and the third with the right),

Figure 38

followed by Play Guitar and then a final Brush Knee, Twist Step attacking with the right palm. When you are attacking with the right palm, the left foot is forward, and when you are attacking with the left palm, the right foot is forward.

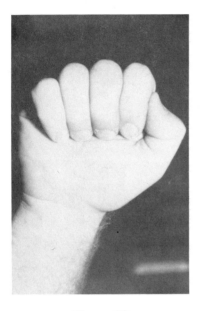

Figure 39

Figure 40

Step Forward, Parry, and Punch

With the weight on your left foot, you turn your left toes 45 degrees to face the southwest. At the same time, the right palm makes a taiji fist (loosely held with the thumb pressing lightly into the second or third bone of the first finger, as in fig. 39) and turns palm down. As you do this, the left palm turns upward (fig. 40).

Inhale and take your right fist down across to the left side of your body in an arc so that the fingers of the left palm are now pointing into the hole that your right fist makes. Now, as in Figure 41, both palms lift up to ear height; the left palm has turned to face downward, and the right foot has lifted to step to the west.

Block downward with the back of your right arm—palm up, still holding a fist—and step to the west with the toes of the right foot pointing slightly northwest. As shown in Figure 42, bring your right fist to your right hip and, as the weight changes to your right leg, exhale and strike with your left palm.

Figure 41

Figure 42

Figure 43

Figure 44

Figure 45

Now take a step with your left foot to the west and inhale. As the weight moves onto the left foot, exhale and punch with your right fist to the west. You are now in a left "bow" stance (fig. 43). Your left palm has come back to the inside of your right forearm. The knuckles of the right fist and the tips of your left fingers should be in line with the center of your torso.

Sit Back and Push Forward

Slide your left palm under your right forearm while turning the right palm up. The left palm is down. The right elbow is on the left wrist. Leave your left arm where it is and sit back onto your right leg. This will drag your right palm back to your right hip as it turns over to palm up (fig. 44).

Your body is turned slightly to the northwest. Circle the right palm up to the level of the left palm, which has turned out away from you as your torso turns back to face west. Now, as shown in Figure 45, push forward and squeeze your elbows in slightly as you shift forward and bend the left knee. Exhale.

Apparent Close-Up

Holding the palms as they are, lift your elbows slightly as you sit back onto your right leg and inhale (fig. 46). Turn your left toes 90 degrees to the north, and turn the whole body to face north.

Shift the weight back to the left leg and move the arms to make two large circles in front of you. The right palm traces a clockwise circle while the left traces a counterclockwise circle. As this is happening, pull the right foot back so that it is parallel to the left foot. As your arms cross in front of your chest, you change your weight to your right leg (fig. 47). Exhale.

*   *   *   *   *

Figure 46

Figure 47

Figure 48

Figure 49

THE "ORIGINAL" YANG CH'ENG-FU FORM: PART TWO

Embrace Tiger, Return to Mountain

With your weight still on your right foot, turn your left toes 45 degrees to the right to point northeast. Shift your weight onto your left leg as your left palm drops under your right to hold a large ball (fig. 48). Inhale.

Now perform the right-foot-forward version of Brush Knee, Twist Step exactly as you did earlier, the only difference being that your right foot steps right around into the Southeast (fig. 49). You brush the right knee with your right thumb and the weight is now on your right leg. Exhale.

Grasping Swallow's Tail

Some of the postures done in the first section are duplicated here. First, raise your right palm up in front of your left palm and inhale.

Pull Back

Repeat the movements in

Figure 17, only facing southeast (fig. 50).

Chee
Repeat the movements
shown in Figure 18, only facing southeast.

Sit Back
Repeat the movements
shown in Figure 19, only facing southeast.

Press Forward
Repeat the movements
shown in Figure 20 only facing southeast.

Figure 50

Sit Back, Ready
Repeat the movements
shown in Figure 21, only facing southeast.

Fishes in Eight
Repeat the movements in
Figures 22 and 23; however,
the direction for each turn is
first to the north and then to
the east.

Push to the Northwest
Holding the palms in the
Fishes in Eight configuration,
you now take a step with your
left foot around into the
northwest corner while inhal-

Figure 51

Figure 52

ing. Roll your weight forward onto your left foot and bring the left palm, which was pointing in to the right elbow, up beside the right palm to perform a pushing movement into the northwest corner (fig. 51). The back toes come around 45 degrees to point to the north. Exhale.

Fist Under Elbow

Bring your right foot up parallel to your left; the feet should be shoulder-width distance apart. You should now be standing on a southwest to northeast diagonal and facing to the northwest with the weight on your left foot. Inhale.

As you shift your weight onto your left leg, make a fist with your right hand and move it across your body in a shallow arc so that it ends up under your left elbow. The tip of the left elbow sits in the "cup" created by the fist being loosely held. At the same time you should turn your body to the west and make a heel stance, empty of weight, with the left foot as you exhale (fig. 52). The left index finger is aligned with the nose.

Figure 53

Step Back, Repulse Monkey

Open both palms so that they face up. Inhale as you take your right palm back to the northeast corner, palm down (fig. 53). Your body turns to the right slightly so that you are able to see the right palm out of the corners of your eyes.

Take a step behind to the southeast with your left foot and place it so that the toe touches first. (When weighted, that foot's toes should point to the southwest.) As you sit back on the left leg, the right palm comes past your ear as the left palm does an arc down to your left hip. The palms pass each other in the front of your body as you sit back. Exhale and turn your right toes to the west once there is no longer any weight on the right leg. The wrist remains relaxed until the final movement when it strikes and flexes (fig. 54).

Next, turn your right palm over and now take your left palm back in the same way as you did with the right one and inhale (fig. 55).

Take a step with your right foot to the rear, and as the weight goes back onto it

Figure 54

Figure 55

Figure 56

Figure 57

the left palm strikes as the right palm blocks in the same way as before, only reversed (fig. 56). Exhale.

Turn the left palm over and repeat this on the right side again so that the right palm is striking, as in Figure 54. Repeat again on the left side so that the left palm is striking, as in Figures 55 and 56.

One last time, repeat on the right and finish up with the right palm striking and the right foot forward still facing to the west, as in Figure 54.

You have now performed five repetitions of this posture: right, left, right, left, right.

Stroking Horse's Mane

With the weight on your left leg, drop the right palm down and bring the left palm up on top as if holding a large ball at the top and bottom, still facing to the west. Swing your leg around to the northeast corner with your right heel and place it into that corner. Now swivel on your heels as you change your weight onto the right foot, and sweep your right arm to point to the northeast as your left arm goes back down to your left side (fig. 57).

Your right heel and your left toes should be in line. Inhale when you hold the ball and exhale as you sweep the right arm.

Lift Hands

Repeat the movements in Figure 27, except that you are facing a different direction in the beginning. As you lift both palms up as if your arms were wings, inhale and turn your left toes 45 degrees so that they point to the northwest. As you place your weight onto the left leg, lift your palms in front of you as before and exhale as you finish.

Pull Down

Repeat the movements in Figure 28.

Shoulder Press

Repeat the movements in Figure 29.

Stork Spreads Wings

Repeat the movements in Figures 30 and 31.

Hold the Ball

Repeat the movements in Figure 32.

Brush Knee, Twist Step (Left Foot Forward)

Repeat the movements in Figures 33 and 34.

Figure 58

Golden Needle at Sea Bottom

Pick up the right foot and put it down on the same spot in a "false step," as you did in the first section in the posture of Stork Spreads Wings. Shift the weight back onto the right leg. As you inhale, the left foot is dragged slightly to the right to gain a "toe stance," as the torso bends downward so that the fingers of the right palm point to the ground (fig. 58). Exhale. Do not curve the back.

The eyes look straight ahead and not at the floor. Your left palm does not move.

Fan through the Back

Inhale as you straighten up again. This also lifts your right palm up to a lateral position. The palm starts to turn over so that it is facing downward (fig. 59).

Figure 59

Take a step with your left foot diagonally and forward to the west (to the same position as for Brush Knee, Twist Step). As your weight is placed onto your left foot, the right palm pulls back, facing away from your right ear while the left fingers poke upward (fig. 60). Exhale.

Turn Around and Chop with Fist

Using a weighted turn, the left toes turn 90 degrees to face the north. At the same time, make a fist with the right hand and bring it down in a clockwise circle until the thumb is pointing to the solar plexus (fig. 61). The left palm moves over your head in a warding-off action with the palm facing out. Inhale.

Figure 60

Figure 61

Figure 62

Figure 63

Bring the right fist up to behind the left palm; at the same time swing the right leg around to the east and shift forward onto the bent right knee. Chop downward with the right fist until it arrives at your right hip while the left palm attacks to the east (fig. 62). Inhale.

Upper Cut, Step Forward, Parry, and Punch

The right fist now punches straight upward as if punching under the chin. (Pause in your breathing.) The fist now turns down as the left palm turns up (fig. 63).

Inhale as both palms come down to your left side and then rise again up to your left ear, as your right foot picks up and is placed down again in front on the heel. The toes of that foot should be turned 45 degrees to the southeast. This is the same posture as at the end of the first section (fig. 42).

The left palm is attacking forward while the right is at your right hip. Now, as in Figure 43, you should step to the east and, as the weight comes down onto your left leg, perform a straight punch.

Diagonal P'eng

From the last posture, your left palm slides under your right forearm, only this time both palms are facing down. Keeping the weight on your left leg, turn your left toes to the northeast and slide your left palm out to that corner in a warding-off action, as in Figure 64. Inhale as you slide your arm under and exhale as you perform P'eng.

Grasping Swallow's Tail

Now repeat the same postures we performed in the first section. First, bring the right palm under your left palm and inhale (fig. 65). Now step to the east with your right foot and perform: Double Ward-Off, as in Figure 16; Pull Back, as in Figure 17; Chee, as in Figure 18; Sit Back, as in Figure 19; and Press Forward as in Figure 20.

Sit Back, Ready

Repeat the movements depicted in Figure 21.

Fishes in Eight

Repeat the movements depicted in Figures 22 and 23.

Figure 64

Figure 65

Figure 66

Figure 67

Single Whip

Repeat the movements in Figures 24 and 25.

NOTE: You are now facing west. There is only one occasion when Single Whip points to a direction other than the west, and that is at the beginning of the third section.

Wave Hands Like Clouds

Using a weighted turn, turn the left foot 90 degrees to the right to point to the north. Inhale. At the same time, bring the left palm across in front of your forehead and into the northwest corner. Also, at the same time, flex your right palm and bring it down and across in an arc directly under the left palm (fig. 66).

Push the left palm down on the outside of the right one with the palm facing downward while the right one comes up the inside as if rubbing your stomach (fig. 67). Simultaneously, the right foot is dragged back, parallel to the left foot as you exhale. Your body still faces the northwest.

Turn your torso to the northeast and change your weight to your right leg.

Reverse the hand movements you just did, i.e., the right palm pushes down as the left palm rubs the stomach, as you inhale and take a double shoulder-width step to your left (fig. 68).

NOTE: This is your second step, counting the first time you pulled the right foot back. There are nine steps and palm changes to make.

Figure 68

Turn your torso to the northwest corner, holding your palms in that same position, left up and right down. Now, change your palms again, left down and right up as you drag your right foot up to single shoulder-width as you exhale (fig. 69). This is your third step. Your right palm is now on the top.

From here you repeat the turn to the northeast and the change with the step, as in Figure 68. This is your fourth step.

Turn to the northwest, step, and change, as in Figure 69. This is your fifth step.

Turn to the northeast, step, and change, as in Figure 68. This is your sixth step.

Figure 69

Figure 70

Turn to the northwest, step, and change, as in Figure 69. This is your seventh step.

Turn to the northeast, step, and change, as in Figure 68. This is your eighth step.

Turn to the northwest, step and change, as in Figure 69. This is your ninth and final step.

As in Figure 70, you now turn back to the northeast with your right palm on the top and bring your left palm up with the fingers pointing to the inside of your right elbow. Inhale.

Single Whip

Repeat the movements shown in Figure 25.

Lift Up the Heavens

As in Figure 71, sit back onto your right leg and turn both palms up as if holding two plates. Inhale.

Figure 71

High Pat on Horse

The right palm pushes past your right ear toward the west with the fingers pointing toward the head. At the same time, the left palm does a clockwise arc down the front of your body to end up at your left hip (fig. 72). The left foot is dragged back and makes a toe stance, no weight on that leg, as you exhale.

Drawing the Bow (Right)

Cross your right palm over your left forearm. The right palm is facing down while the left is up. The circle continues as the left palm crosses over the inside of your right forearm (fig. 73). As this is happening the left foot takes a step to the southwest corner as you inhale.

Figure 72

Figure 73

Figure 74

As you transfer your weight to your left foot, pull the left palm back to your left ear as you attack into the northwest corner with the right palm as if you are drawing a bow (fig. 74). Exhale.

Separation of Right Leg (Right Instep Kick)

Move your right palm down in an arc across your body and up to cross over your left forearm, palms toward you. (If you kick with the right foot, the right palm is on the outside; this is reversed for the left foot.) As your arms come up to cross, your right foot comes up as you inhale (fig. 75).

Figure 75

As shown in Figure 76, turn your palms outward as you push them out to the south and northwest. Straighten your left leg as this happens and exhale.

As soon as your arms are in position and your left leg is straight, you kick your right foot out to the northwest corner as you inhale (fig. 77). The foot and hand should not reach out together, nor should there be a long wait before the foot kicks. The foot reaches its goal a split second after the right palm is in position.

Figure 76

Figure 77

Figure 78

Drawing the Bow (Left)

From the last position, turn your right palm over and, as you step to the northwest corner, circle your left palm in to touch the inside of your right elbow. This happens as the right heel touches the ground. Now the left palm circles out, as in Figure 78, to form the Drawing Bow posture exactly as before, only reversed. Exhale on the down step and up to the end of "holding" the bow.

Separation of Left Leg (Left Instep Kick)

Reversing the previous posture, cross the arms in front of you and open the palms out to the southwest and to the north, as shown in Figure 79. Perform the kick with the instep of the left foot. Inhale.

On completion of this kick, bring the left foot back in to the right knee, which has bent downward again. The arms are as they were for the kick.

Figure 79

Spin Around and Kick with Heel

You must now use the swinging momentum of your left foot to spin yourself around on your right heel so that the toes on that foot point to the south. Your arms crossed at the wrists with the natural flow of the movement. The left toes are off the ground, and your body is facing to the southeast (fig. 80).

As part of that exhalation, lift your left knee as your palms open and push out as before. (All of the kicks start the same way.)

As shown in Figure 81, inhale as you kick with your left heel to the east.

Figure 80

Figure 81

Figure 82

Finish by bending your right leg and laying your left elbow across your left knee, as shown in Figure 82. The right palm relaxes. This is part of your exhalation.

Brush Knee, Twist Step (Left Foot Forward)

Brush your left knee with your left palm as you step to the east with your left foot. Strike with your right palm as you exhale (fig. 83). Your right toes come around by 45 degrees.

Figure 83

Brush Knee, Twist Step (Right Foot Forward)

This is a repetition of the weighted turn variation of this posture you did in the first section of the form. Turn the left foot out 45 degrees to the northeast and hold the ball on the left with the right palm on the top. As shown in Figure 84, brush your right knee and step with the right leg to the east as you attack with your left palm.

Strike the Triple Warmer Points

Some teachers call this posture Punch to Knee. Turn your right foot, weighted, 45 degrees to the southeast, and place your fist onto your right knee (fig. 85). You must bend slightly for this, but do not curve your back. Bring the left palm over as if holding the ball. Inhale.

Figure 84

Figure 85

Figure 86

Figure 87

Step to the east with your left foot and, as the knee comes through, brush it as you would in Brush Knee, Twist Step. As the body weight shifts onto the left foot, the right fist naturally swings forward (fig. 86). Exhale.

Turn Around and Chop with Fist

Repeat the movements in Figure 61, except your final action is to the west, attacking with your left palm and right foot forward as in Figure 62.

Uppercut, Step Forward, Parry, and Punch

Repeat the movements shown in Figure 63, except the direction is to the west. Punch upward and turn the left palm over with the right fist down.

Pull down to your left, bring both palms up to your ear, and punch down with your right fist across your body as you strike with your left palm to the west, as in Figure 42.

Step through to the west with your left foot and punch with your right fist, as in Figure 43.

Diagonal P'eng

This is the same as the one performed earlier, only to the southwest. Slide your left palm under your right wrist and p'eng into the southwest corner as your left foot swivels to the southwest. The right palm comes down to your right side. The only difference this time is that you now look at your right palm as it strikes (fig. 87).

Figure 88

Right Heel Kick

Circle your right arm back up to be across the left forearm as for any of the kicks. Inhale. Push the palms out to the northwest and south as you kick to the northwest with your right heel (fig. 88). Exhale as you push your palms out and inhale as you kick.

Attack to the Right

Exhale as you put the right foot down exactly parallel to the left foot and point the right thumb to your breastbone (fig. 89). Leave the left palm as it was at the end of the kick. You are now facing to the southwest corner and your feet are on the southeast to northwest diagonal.

Figure 89

Figure 90

Continue to exhale as you push the right palm to the west and change the weight to the right foot (fig. 90). The left palm comes across your chest to replace the right.

Hit Tiger, Left

Turn the left palm over and step to the southeast corner with the left foot as you inhale. As the weight rolls on to the left foot, bring the left palm across your body to the left and form fists with both palms. Exhale as you punch. The left fist is uppermost and directly above the right fist. Both hands are aligned with the center of the torso. Pull the right foot around 45 degrees (pivoting on the heel) so that the toes point to the south (fig. 91).

Figure 91

Hit Tiger, Right

Using a weighted turn, turn the left toes 90 degrees to the southwest and open the right palm, which faces upward. As shown in Figure 92, the left palm simultaneously wards off at the left temple. Inhale.

Lift the right foot and put it down into the northwest corner. As you shift your weight onto it, bring your right palm down and across your body as before. When your right palm is parallel to the ground, form two fists and strike as before, only the right fist is on top (fig. 93). Exhale.

Figure 92

Figure 93

Figure 94

Phoenix Punch and Turn

As part of the last exhalation, bring the left fist up beside the right as you simultaneously turn your left foot to the south and change your weight onto it as you swivel the right foot around on the heel so that the toes point to the southwest (fig. 94).

Kick with Right Heel

Open both palms and circle them out and down as you inhale. Bring both palms back up to cross in front as for all of the kicks, right palm on the outside. Push the right palm out to the west and the left out to the southeast, and kick with your right heel to the west. (This is the same as Figure 88, only to the west.)

Double Wind Goes through Ears

From that last kick, turn both palms over and let them fall and brush both sides of your right knee (fig. 95).

Figure 95

Exhale as you step down into the northwest corner and perform this posture. Both palms sweep downward and circle back up (fig. 96).

Drag the left foot around 90 degrees to point to the west. The right foot points to the northwest. Open both palms and circle them to cross left over right ready for the kick. As before, push both palms out and kick with your left heel to the west (fig. 97).

Figure 96

Figure 97

Figure 98

Spin Around and Kick

Use the swinging momentum of your left leg as a lever to cause you to spin around on the ball of your right foot. Your left foot lands with the weight placed to the rear and the toes pointing to the southwest. You are still facing to the west as your palms cross in front of you, right over left (fig. 98).

Right Heel Kick

Open both palms as before and kick to the northwest with your right heel as you inhale (fig. 99).

Figure 99

Step Forward, Parry, and Punch

Perform this exactly as you did at the end of the first section of the form. From the last kick, place your right elbow onto your right knee (fig. 100).

Exhale as you circle your right fist up to your left ear and repeat the movements in Figure 42. Step through and punch with your right fist, as in Figure 43.

Sit Back and Push Forward

Repeat the movements depicted in Figures 44 and 45.

Figure 100

Apparent Close-Up

Repeat the movements shown in Figures 46 and 47.

*   *   *   *   *

THE "ORIGINAL" YANG CH'ENG-FU FORM:
PART THREE

Embrace Tiger, Return to Mountain
This is exactly the same as at the beginning of the second section (figs. 48 and 49), except you are going toward the southeast and not to the east.

Sit Back, Ready
Repeat the movements in Figure 50.

Pull Back
Repeat the movements in Figure 17.

Chee
Repeat the movements in Figure 18.

Sit Back and Press Forward
Repeat the movements in Figures 19 and 20.

Sit Back, Ready
Repeat the movements in Figure 21.

Fishes in Eight
Repeat the actions as in the beginning of the second section (fig. 22), except first to the north and then to the east.

Diagonal Single Whip
From Fishes in Eight, you now perform Single Whip (instead of Push to the Northwest, as in the second section), as in Figures 24 and 25, ending up to the northwest.

Slant Flying (Right Leg Forward)
Turn your left leg—a weighted turn—90 degrees to point northeast. At the same time, hold a ball with your right palm

underneath (fig. 101). Inhale.

Take a step into the southeast corner with your right foot, the toes pointing to the southwest. As you change your weight onto the right leg, exhale as you cut up with your right palm and push down with your left palm (fig. 102). Your right wrist is in your center, and your right elbow is over your right knee. Your left toes turn to the east.

Figure 101

Figure 102

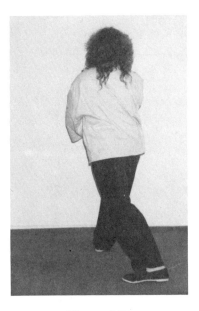

Figure 103

Slant Flying (Left Foot Forward)

From the last position, turn your right toes to the south in a weighted turn as you inhale and hold the ball with your right palm on the top (fig. 103).

Now, as before, only to the opposite direction, step to the northeast corner with your left foot, and, as the weight is transferred onto your right foot, slant upward with your left palm as your right one goes back down to your right side (fig. 104). Your right toes are dragged around to the east. Exhale.

Slant Flying (Right Foot Forward)

As before (fig. 102), hold the ball with your left palm on the top and turn your left foot, weighted, to the north as you inhale. Step to the southeast corner with your right foot and repeat the posture as you first did it.

Figure 104

Sit Back and Block

From the last position, sit back onto your left foot and block while inhaling (fig. 105).

Turn your right toes 90 degrees to the northeast and then put your weight onto that leg so that you are now facing to the northeast. Take a step with your left foot to the north and perform P'eng exactly as you did it at the beginning of the form (fig. 106).

Grasp Swallow's Tail

Repeat the movements in Figures 15, 16, 17, 18, 19, and 20.

Figure 105

Sit Back, Ready

Repeat the movements in Figure 21.

Fishes in Eight

Repeat the movements in Figures 22 and 23.

Single Whip

Repeat the movements in Figures 24 and 25.

Figure 106

Figure 107

Fair Lady Works at Shuttles

Do a weighted turn on your left heel so that your toes point to the north. As you do this, hold a ball with your left palm underneath (fig. 107). Inhale.

As your wrists cross (palms upward), pick up your right foot and place it down again with the toes pointing to the east (fig. 108).

Figure 108

Place your weight onto your right foot and take your right palm back to your right hip as your left palm rises upward (fig. 109).

Take a step to the northeast corner with your left foot and, as your weight moves onto it, your left palm turns outward while your right palm circles upward to strike to the northeast near your left palm. (fig. 110).

Figure 109

Figure 110

Figure 111

From here you have to repeat this posture into the northwest corner. First, push downward with your right palm as your left leg swivels in a weighted turn right around to point to the south. Inhale as you hold a ball with the right palm underneath (fig. 111).

Cross your wrists as before only with the right under and step into the northwest corner, as your left palm comes down to your left side and your right palm wards off (fig. 112).

Figure 112

As in Figure 113, roll your weight onto your right foot as your left palm strikes (weight still on your right leg).

Hold a ball, left palm underneath (fig. 114).

Figure 113

Figure 114

Figure 115

Cross your wrists as before, left under right, and step into the southwest corner with your left foot, as your right palm comes down to your right side and your left palm wards off. Roll onto your left leg as you strike with your right palm to the southwest (fig. 115).

Now you must repeat exactly the same movements as in Figures 110, 111, and 112. You have now performed this posture into the four corners, starting with the northeast, then the northwest, the southwest, and the southeast.

The last set of movements went from the southwest corner into the southeast corner, but the photos are the same as from the northeast corner to the northwest corner. You finish up as in Figure 116.

Sit Back and Block

Repeat the movements in Figures 105 and 106.

Grasp Swallow's Tail

Repeat the movements in Figures 15, 16, 17, 18, 19, and 20.

Figure 116

Sit Back, Ready
Repeat the movements in Figure 21.

Fishes in Eight
Repeat the movements in Figures 22 and 23.

Single Whip
Repeat the movements in Figures 24 and 25.

Wave Hands Like Clouds
Repeat the movements in Figures 66, 67, 68, 69, and 70.

Single Whip
Repeat the movements in Figure 25.

Snake Creeps Down
Many instructors call this posture Squatting Single Whip. Turn your right toes to the northeast, then turn out the heel so that the toes point to the northwest. Then turn the toes again northeast so that you have shuffled your foot to the rear and are in a much wider stance. Drop down onto your right leg so that the knee of the right leg is over the right toes. The left foot has adjusted itself so that the toes point to the northwest. Both feet are flat on the ground.

Inhale as you shuffle backward and exhale as you squat down. The right palm stays as for Single Whip while the left drops. Keep the back straight (fig. 117).

Figure 117

Figure 118

Golden Cock Stands on Left Leg

As you shift your weight forward onto your left leg, turn your left toes out 90 degrees to point southwest. Drag the toes of the right foot forward so that they point to the northwest. The left palm is poking forward while the fingers of the right palm open up (fig. 118).

Continuing, bring your right palm downward in an arc, and, as it subsequently rises, stand up in one sweeping movement. Don't drag the toes on the ground; the right foot should turn as much as possible to allow for this. As in Figure 119, bring your right elbow to your right knee and your left palm back down to your left side. Inhale.

Figure 119

Golden Cock Stands on Right Leg

Take a small step to the rear with your right foot and take your right palm down to your right side, then bring your left knee and palm upward as in Figure 120, so that your left elbow is now on your left knee—the exact opposite of the previous posture. Exhale as you step down and inhale as you lift your knee.

Step Back, Repulse Monkey

Repeat the same group of movements performed in the second section. Bring your right palm upward so that it is near your left elbow and turn both palms up as you finish the last exhalation (fig. 121).

Figure 120

Take your right palm back to the northeast corner and, as you step to the rear with your left foot, repeat the movements from Figures 53, 54, 55, and 56.

NOTE: This time you do only three Repulse Monkeys instead of five. You still end up with your right foot and palm forward.

Figure 121

Stroking Wild Horse's Mane
Repeat the movements shown in Figure 57.

Lift Hands
Repeat the movements in Figures 26 and 27.

Pull-Down
Repeat the movements shown in Figure 28.

Shoulder Stroke
Repeat the movements in Figure 29.

Stork Spreads Wings
Repeat the movements in Figures 30 and 31.

Brush Knee, Twist Step (Left Foot Forward)
Repeat the movements in Figures 32, 33, and 34.

Grasp the Golden Needle at Sea Bottom
Repeat the movements in Figure 58.

Fan through Back
Repeat the movements in Figures 59 and 60.

White Snake Puts Out Tongue
This time there is a slight difference in that the posture called Turn Around and Chop with Fist is repeated, as in Figures 61 and 62, except that the right hand remains open and does not form a fist.

Keep going as in the second section, Figures 63, 42, and 43 up to Punch.

Diagonal P'eng
Repeat the movements in Figure 64.

Grasp Swallow's Tail
Repeat the movements you did in the second section,

Figures 65, 16, 17, 18, 19, and 20.

Sit Back, Ready
Repeat the movements in Figure 21.

Fishes in Eight
Repeat the movements in Figures 22 and 23.

Single Whip
Repeat the movements in Figures 24 and 25.

Wave Hands Like Clouds
Repeat the movements in Figures 66, 67, 68, 69, and 70.

Single Whip
Repeat the movements in Figure 25.

Lift Up the Heavens
Repeat the movements in Figure 71.

High Pat on Horse
Repeat the movements in Figure 72.

Inspection of Horse's Mouth
Take a step to your left diagonally to gain a bow stance to the west. As you transfer your weight onto your left foot, slide your left palm over your right wrist all the way up to your elbow, and exhale as you do so (fig. 122).

Figure 122

Figure 123

Cross Over and Kick with Right Heel

Using a weighted turn, the left foot swivels on the heel until the toes turn to the north as your left palm wards off overhead and your right palm guards under your left armpit (fig. 123). Inhale.

Open the palms, right arm to the east and to left arm to the northwest, and kick with your right heel to the east (fig. 124).

Figure 124

Punch to Groin

With the right knee still held up, place your right fist onto the outside of your right knee and take a step forward with your right foot so that your toes are pointing to the southeast. With your right fist still on your right knee, your left palm is holding the ball over the right knee (fig. 125).

Now, as in this same posture in the second section, take a step to the east with your left foot and, at the same time, brush your left knee with your left palm and punch downward to the area of the groin—a little higher than the last time (fig. 126)

Figure 125

Diagonal P'eng

This is almost exactly as you did it in the second section. Cross your left wrist under your right forearm and slide your left palm under your right wrist to end up to the northeast in a ward-off posture (fig. 64).

Grasp Swallow's Tail

Repeat the movements in Figures 65, 15, 16, 17, 18, 19, and 20.

Figure 126

Figure 127

Figure 128

Sit Back, Ready
Repeat the movements in Figure 21.

Fishes in Eight
Repeat the movements in Figures 22 and 23.

Single Whip
Repeat the movements in Figures 24 and 25.

Snake Creeps Down
This posture ends as before, but the beginning is different. As you shuffle backward, bring your right palm down in an arc to just in front of your left (fig. 127).

As you sit down onto your right leg you pull both palms back until the left palm is near your right ear (fig. 128).

Next, make a hook with your right palm and poke your fingers down along the inside of your left thigh (fig. 129).

Step Up to Form Seven Stars

Come back up in the same way as before, but this time as you bring your right foot forward, place it down in a toe stance to the west as you cross your wrists in front holding two fists (fig. 130).

Figure 129

Figure 130

Before my training with Chang Yiu-chun, I was told that this posture was so that we could protect the seven important areas of the body; namely, the head, shoulders, hips, and knees. However, I now know that this is a special qigong posture for opening up the seven

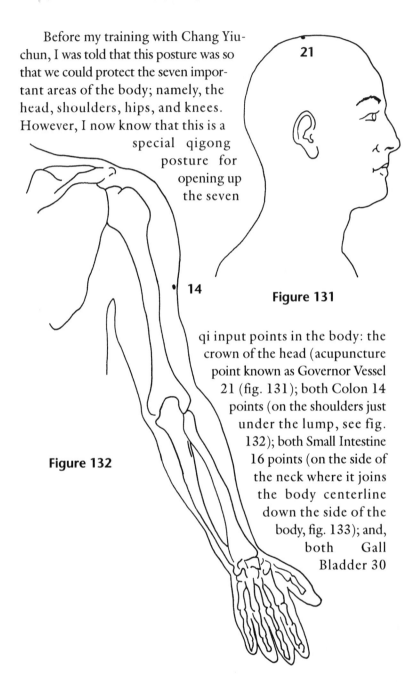

21

14

Figure 131

Figure 132

qi input points in the body: the crown of the head (acupuncture point known as Governor Vessel 21 (fig. 131); both Colon 14 points (on the shoulders just under the lump, see fig. 132); both Small Intestine 16 points (on the side of the neck where it joins the body centerline down the side of the body, fig. 133); and, both Gall Bladder 30 points (in the hollow of the buttocks, fig. 134).

In a nutshell, these points are responsible for taking in "ground energy," which is

Figure 134

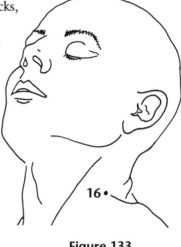

16•

Figure 133

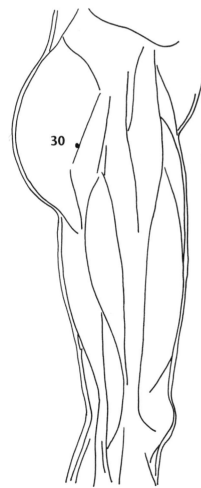

30 •

used for, among other things, communication at higher levels.

Figure 135

Ride Tiger Back to Mountain

From the last posture, open both palms as if holding a small ball and start to take a right step backward (fig. 135).

Inhale as you hold this ball and exhale as you enter the next posture. Place your right foot down, and as you sit back onto it, open both palms in a movement like that in Stork Spreads Wings (fig. 136).

Figure 136

Spin Around and Lotus Kick

Bring your left palm up and your right palm down to meet it at the elbow as shown in Figure 137. Inhale.

Turn your shoulders slightly to your left and as you spin right around on the ball of your right foot, your right palm is pushed out so that you end up in the exact opposite position you started from (fig. 138). The left foot is to the rear and the weight is now placed on it.

Figure 137

Figure 138

Figure 139

Take your palms into the northwest corner by turning your waist. Bring your right foot up in an arc from left to right as both palms strike the right foot as shown in Figure 139. The palms are traveling to the left while the foot is traveling to your right.

Your right foot ends up in the northwest corner with toes facing to the northwest. Your palms continue the counter-clockwise circle to end up over your right knee (fig. 140).

Inhale as you kick, and exhale for the next posture.

Figure 140

Phoenix Punch

Lift both palms up so that they form two fists facing each other, as in Figure 141.

Shoot Tiger

Turn your hips slightly to your right as your left fist strikes downward and your right fist moves over your head. This is also part of your last exhalation (fig. 142).

Figure 141

Figure 142

Figure 143

Figure 144

Step Forward, Parry, and Punch

Turn your left palm over as you turn your left foot back to the southwest. As in Figure 143, your right fist follows your left palm as it rises in an arc to your left ear while your right foot lifts up.

Now, as before (fig. 42), step down with your right foot, block, and strike to the west with your left palm.

Step through and punch as in Figure 43.

Sit Back and Push Forward

Repeat the movements exactly as in the earlier sections (figs. 44 and 45).

Apparent Close-Up

Repeat the movements exactly as in the first and second sections (figs. 46 and 47)

Conclusion

You have now finished up with your weight on your right leg and arms crossed over your chest (fig. 144).

Lower both palms to your lower abdomen as you allow yourself to be double-weighted. As you raise your palms to shoulder height, inhale and lower your weight as low as you can go, still keeping your back vertical (fig. 145).

Push down with both palms as you straighten your legs and exhale. You are now in the same position you began with, which is also the end of the whole original Yang Cheng-fu taijiquan slow form.

Figure 145

CONCLUSION

It is now up to you to practice, practice, and practice some more. Don't expect to do everything perfectly; just try to get the movements right and be able to practice them without thinking.

Try to allow your breath to move naturally with each movement and relax your head, really paying attention to your neck and shoulders and relaxing them. Staying as relaxed as possible is the main thing in the beginning.

As you improve, try to concentrate on only one main principle (i.e., avoiding being double-weighted) at a time and see how your whole form changes. Gradually, you will have learned to incorporate all of the main principles into your form.

As you progress, you will begin to understand the old written classics intuitively, and they will teach you. True taijiquan is subconscious; the body and mind enter an "alpha" state, which is neither asleep nor awake. Allow your subconscious to do the work for you and you can achieve almost anything.

It takes many years to achieve a high level of taijiquan, but on the way you will come across wondrous things and learn valuable lessons about yourself and life. To make progress, you must "invest in loss."

No teacher can give you taijiquan; all he or she can do is show you the movements and then allow you to teach yourself. Be your own master!

chapter three

Though there are more advanced ways of doing push-hands, or as we in the Montaigue system like to call it, "joining-arms," the following methods are the foundation of your martial taiji practice.

However, even our basics are, in many ways, much more challenging than what is normally taught today as advanced push-hands. Few instructors know about the "joining arms" methods of P'eng and Hinge, Small Circle, and Small Circle Ch'in-na—much less teach them.

Push-hands is the culmination of what you have learned by practicing the slow form and qigong in terms of energy creation and usage. We learn to distinguish between yin and yang with reference to an oncoming force and how to deal with the attack without using too much energy.

As your external body becomes more and more sensitive, so too do the internal and your mind. When the internal becomes more aware, this helps the external, and so on. So each step we take helps us up the ladder to our goal, whatever that may be.

I hope that each student will use the methods outlined in this chapter to experiment, finding new directions and ways of doing things.

BASICS OF PUSH-HANDS AND RELATED METHODS

IMPORTANT POINTS

At an advanced stage, anything can happen in push-hands as long as you keep all of the important principles of taijiquan in mind! However, as with the form, there are some basic rules you must follow when practicing push-hands as a beginner.

1) Always keep your wrist aligned with the center of your body, turning your body and arm to achieve this.

2) Never allow your wrist to come too close to your chest. Hold the wrist as if you have a wheel in front of you. When a force is attacking that wheel, it just turns on its axis and throws the attack away.

3) Keep your back vertical and do not lean backward for the sake of yielding to an attack. This may well allow you to get away from the attack, but it builds a bad martial habit. Maintain your center and turn the spine as your axis.

4) Only attack when your partner has made a mistake and you are able to take advantage of it. Anyone can use brute strength. The idea is not to show your partners how strong you are or how easily you can push them over, but rather to develop sensitivity. We only push each other to help each other up the ladder. Doing otherwise will cause us to lose the whole initial idea of taiji, that of "nonego."

5) Follow the movement; do not try to force your opponent to go in a certain direction. If he or she pushes to the right, you go to the right; if he or she pushes to the left, you go to the left.

6) Never allow your breathing to become rapid or labored; sink your energy to the lower tan-tien and breathe naturally.

7)   Do not practice push-hands for the sake of doing push-hands. It is not an end in itself but rather a means to an end. Always keep in mind that you are using push-hands to increase your martial and healing ability.

8)   If you think that your push-hands is good and you pride yourself on not being able to be pushed over, start from the beginning again because you have not learned taijiquan. You must use this exercise to help each other to understand some very important principles of taiji. If it becomes a competition, then you are only learning push-hands and not taijiquan.

9)   Single push-hands has more to offer than first meets the eye. Look into its real meaning. Do not be too hasty to go on to the more advanced double push-hands and da-lu.

10)   If an attack is too strong, take a step away from it to defeat it. There will always be someone who is physically stronger, so learn to move away from the incoming force rather than trying to meet it head-on. The kind of softness that is used in taijiquan is not floppy or limp but rather like the yielding you find in a metal spring. The spring will give way only to a certain point and then bounce back with great energy. (In the beginning we do try to withstand attacks using the metal spring principle, but this is only to make us stronger. The "old masters" were already strong from decades of training, so we have to regain that "strength" before learning taijiquan.)

Using the Right Muscles for the Right Job

To make the best use of your given physical strength, you must know how to use only the amount of muscle necessary for that particular work.

In particular, you must know how to relax countermuscles.

For instance, you do not want to use your biceps muscles if you are pushing or your triceps if you are pulling.

Lean up against a wall with the back of one of your palms touching the wall. Lift one foot off the ground so that there is a lot of pressure on the arm. Now feel the biceps of your supporting arm; it should be totally relaxed.

Next, grab some object that is attached to something solid with one hand and lean backward with your arm slightly bent as before. Now your triceps should be totally relaxed when you feel it with your free hand.

Using Qi

Although qi is quite indefinable, if you follow all of the main points of qigong and taijiquan, you should start to feel something new.

I have witnessed seemingly supernatural feats, most of which later proved to be fake. However, a few did defy rational explanation. It is the one in a million that I have seen that makes me believe that there is something "extra" to be gained from your training. Even if it is just great good health, what more can you ask for?

With a little more training, you might just find out something else. The main idea is not to start taijiquan and qigong to become a superman. If this is your idea, you will never succeed, as the following story illustrates.

> *A young man in Japan wanted to study swordplay with a famous master, so he asked the master how long it would take him to learn the sword if he practiced every day. The master told him about 25 years. The boy looked shocked and asked how long it would take him if he practiced night and day and had mastership as his only goal. The master told him that he would never learn!*

WHAT THE MASTERS SAY

I believe that, when it comes to any aspect of life, one should experience it for oneself to really appreciate its lessons. It's just not good enough to take some master's word for things if we do not actually understand them ourselves.

My main teacher, Chang Yiu-chun, said over and over, "Stop asking questions; learn it yourself." Someone had to invent all the martial arts, and there had to be a time when all the various systems were new and not classical.

In the fine arts, something only becomes a "classic" after many years of use. Even then, it must be accepted by the public to achieve that status.

It's the same with the martial arts. A style only becomes a classical style after many years of continued and tested use. But does that also necessarily make it good? Perhaps thousands of people are practicing something that is flawed simply because they have taken the word of the inventor and never questioned its truth.

So often we hear th question, "Is it a classical style?" This implies that it must not be good if it is not. We never stop to think that, at one time, *all* styles must have been new styles yet to be tested.

Taiji and all of the other "internal" styles have a built-in mechanism that allows us to still practice the style as times change. Many of the ancient styles were built around the self-defense needs of their time, when people roamed the streets with swords hanging by their sides or there was a real likelihood of being attacked with a spear.

Such is not usually the case in modern times, and, to remain a viable martial art, any system must be able to evolve to suit the times. For example, I know of karate katas in which the foot is slapped against the floor during their practice. No one knew for many years exactly what this slap meant until a friend of mine went to Okinawa and found out that it represented taking off the wooden "shoe" worn decades ago, to throw it at an attacker! Those shoes are obsolete, but the move is still in the kata.

Only at a high level of development will all of the great benefits of push-hands be available. In fact, I know of so-called "masters" who have been doing the basic push-hands for more than 30 years, never knowing that there is anything above this. Sadly, they have gained little because they took their instructors' word that "it will all work out in the long run."

What use is a martial art if we are only able to use it when we are 90? What use is a healing art if it does not heal us until it is too late?

Push-hands is the basis of taijiquan as a martial art as well as a healing art. By joining hands with a partner, we learn to "feel" another person's movements and to listen with our skin. We learn to know about the center—where it is and how to find it.

In this way, the whole body becomes highly sensitized, and we know intuitively just where and when an attack will occur. There is nothing supernatural about this; it's just that we work with other people for so long that we begin to know certain signs. For example, we learn to feel the changes in potential in the various acupuncture points and are able to find them more easily.

For all of the above to take place, we must practice push-hands the "right way." Everyone is different, but the masters have left us certain guidelines gained from many years of trial and error.

One must keep in mind, however, that what the masters called "push-hands" actually refers to the advanced method of "joining arms"—not the modern push-hands, which teaches us little beyond how to move in coordination with a partner.

The following are translations of the masters' teachings. Most have been translated for me from the old texts written in Chinese. The part from Yang Sau-chung, however, comes directly from him.

Yang Sau-chung

Yang Sau-chung (1909–1985) was the eldest of the four sons of Yang Ch'eng-fu and the teacher of one of my main teachers. I became one of the few Westerners to be introduced formally to Yang. He said the following:

- "Keep yourself balanced; drop your shoulders and elbows naturally, push hard using the connection of the waist and leg, see your opponent and at the same time hollow your chest and raise the back."

- "The strength comes from the whole body and not just the arms. Do not use force, but the idea is there. Shift your center of gravity as required; action and what you are thinking should be in harmony."

- "Loosen the waist. The opponent must turn your waist, you must not turn it. After a while a potential energy will develop and can be used to great advantage in attack and defense."

Yang Ch'eng-fu

Yang Ch'eng-fu (1883–1936), grandson of the founder of Yang taiji, was responsible for de-emphasizing the martial side of the art and changing his father's form into something that anyone could learn. This helped spread taiji, but it also harmed the art in that his style became so easy to learn and widespread that people nowadays think that it embodies the Yang style.

He wrote the following (from *The Art of Taijiquan*, Chen Wei-ming, 1925):

- "The head should be held vertical so that the spirit can reach the crown. Sink the chest naturally and raise up the back." [This does not mean being hunchbacked. When the chest is concave, the back is lifted naturally. Relax the waist; it is the director of the movement and can't do its job if it is tense.]

- "Know the difference between yin and yang; your step will be lively and full of energy. Sink the shoulders and elbows. If this happens you are able to use fa-jing [explosive energy] to great advantage. Use the mind and not force. The whole body should act as a whole unit."

- "The qi is joined without breaks. When we use force to attack there is a time when the power is broken waiting for the body to gain control again. At this time we could be easily attacked. When we use the power of the mind the qi is never broken but flows on and circulates back inward, leaving no openings."

Yang Pan-hou

Yang Pan-hou (1837–1892) was the uncle of Yang Ch'eng-fu and, apart from the latter's brother Yang Shao-hou and Shao-hou's student Chang Yiu-chun, was probably the last great Yang master to teach the original Yang style as a full martial art.

What Pan-hou has to say is more obviously martial in tone than many of the others (from *The Nine Transmission of Taijiquan* and from direct transmission to Chang Yiu-chun):

- "In P'eng both arms should be rounded with a distance between the wrist and chest. [The arms are as if being held up. Whether active or inactive, the idea is always there for attack.] First we use Roll Back then Squeeze Forward; this leaves not much room for escape."

- "Elbow and/or shoulder are used if our technique is somewhat lacking and we are pulled or pushed off balance. We need not fear the great technique of the opponent; we move and change to the conditions."

- "Move in close and take the advantage but be careful of your three fronts—hands, eyes, and feet. [Always attack from the side when attacked first. With a little practice most people can develop a strong P'eng, so use Pull Down or Split to defeat this technique.] Always follow up a successful action without delay to finish the confrontation. Control your four sides but look for weaknesses in your opponent's four corners."

- "When using the elbow or shoulder, move in close in order to uproot using little energy. Use the fa-jing to surprise the opponent, then use spinning energy from the side, turning the waist with great speed."

- "If you are close to the opponent and the longer techniques will not work, use shoulder, elbow, and knee. Not knowing about yin and yang is like having a cart without wheels. When you have the opponent 'in your palm' and feel yin, be wary; if you feel yang, then attack."

- "The maximum power of the hands and feet must arrive together from the side which is out of the free circle. To know about the circle we must first of all know about timing."

- "We must use defense then offense, evade and attack simultaneously. If the opponent locks the joints, follow the movement and block the lock. Sink the body to escape from pulling of the wrist and turn the wrist."

Chang Yiu-chun

Chang Yiu-chun (1899–1986) I now regard as my main teacher, although I have had many others.

He was a true warrior and man of the internal. His words matched his external appearance and way of moving—very economical. But like his movement, his words, though few and in bad English, held much greatness.

- "When touching the opponent, think with your skin."

- "You should never hurt anything; let your body do it if it is imperative that you do."

- "If you do not want to be pushed over, then you have already lost."

- "Lose yourself in the movement."

- "Do all Australians think like you?!"

- "Your eyes are open, but closed."

- "Feel your opponent like you feel your woman, tenderly; he attacks and you aren't there."

- "Everything is alive; do not hurt it—walk on the grass and thank it for making your path soft."

- "You eat too much!"

- "You talk too much!"

- "When you do push-hands, be like that tree over there."

SINGLE PUSH-HANDS

For simplicity, I will be AA and my partner, Les Anwyl (short hair), will be BB.

As in Figure 146, AA and BB stand opposite each other with right feet forward in a bow stance. BB has his right palm on AA's right wrist ready to push. Notice that both players have their right wrists in line with their centers.

BB now pushes toward AA's chest as he shifts forward onto his right foot. AA starts to turn to his right as he begins to sit back. AA now completes the movement as he sits back onto his left leg and turns his center to his right, thus successfully redirecting the oncoming force (fig. 147).

NOTE: The wrists draw a circle but never stray from the center of your body. It is the body that draws the circle. Keep your wrist away from your chest by at least 90 degrees in the beginning.

Figure 146

Figure 147

Figure 148

Figure 149

AA turns his right palm out and pushes toward BB's chest as he exhales (fig. 148).

As in Figure 149, BB should turn his body to his right as he sits back onto his left leg to neutralize the attack.

BB now turns his palm over and repeats what AA has just done. This pushing continues with only light pressure between the two wrists until both players have a good feel for the circular movement and use of the waist.

You must not bend your wrist outward; keep it in, toward you. In the beginning, point your fingers toward your opposite shoulder when being pushed. This will ensure that your arm is curved. This is the strongest position with which to resist an incoming force.

Once you are proficient with this type of push-hands, you are then able to try to catch your opponent off guard every now and again by using a slightly harder push. Your opponent must be sensitive enough to detect the push and neutralize it.

When attacking, never forget the yin (retreat). When

retreating, never forget the yang (attack).

Pull Down

The next attacking technique is Pull Down. As your opponent pushes against your wrist, turn your body as before but instead of reattacking with a push, grab the wrist and pull it downward, as in Figure 150.

There are two ways to defend against this type of attack. The first is the correct way, while the second is a backup in case you do something wrong.

The correct way is to never allow anyone to grab

Figure 150

your wrist, so as BB grabs AA's wrist he should turn it over at precisely the right moment and allow his hand to become yin. BB's attacking palm will just slip off, and AA is then able to attack. Remember that your palm must remain yin; do not turn the wrist inward, as this will give your attacker something to hold on to.

Figure 151

The timing is crucial at the point of the attack. If you turn too soon the attacker will be able to grab your wrist; if you turn too late, well, it's just too late. If a situation like this occurs, which means that you have made a mistake, remember the classic saying, "When you have made a mistake, use da-lu." So if you are grabbed on your wrist and are being pulled downward, go with the force and, as you do this, bend your elbow and attack with that elbow or the shoulder (fig. 151).

Shuffle in toward your opponent using the front foot first, or if you are pulled out to your side (in this case to your left), you should step to your left with your left foot, as in Figure 152.

Figure 152

Using the power from that leg, push in diagonally toward the chest (fig. 153).

Changing the Step in Attack

To change step, AA, on being attacked by BB's right palm, lightly controls BB's right palm downward and attacks his face with his left palm as he steps through with his left foot. As Figure 154 shows, AA's right toes have turned out 45 degrees.

Figure 153

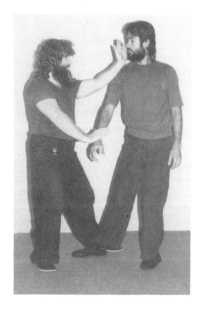

Figure 154

Figure 155

As AA steps through and attacks BB's face, BB takes a right step backward and wards off with his left wrist (fig. 155). The circling can now continue on the opposite side.

Changing the Step to Attack While Stepping Back

Instead of coming forward, AA is able to grab BB's wrist, step backward, and pull BB onto his left palm (fig. 156). BB must step forward and ward off with his left P'eng arm.

Figure 156

Changing the Step Using Low Punch

Instead of using the face attack as before, AA could punch low. AA controls BB's right palm downward as before and turns his right toes out by 45 degrees. AA then steps through and attacks BB's lower right rib area. As in Figure 157, BB should also take a step backward, blocking across with his left forearm and catching the punch with his right forearm on the top of his left.

Figure 157

BB now lifts AA's left arm with his left arm, and the circling continues. So now we have a number of different ways of attack and defense during single push-hands. Push, pull, punch and attack, pull and attack, and low punch can all be used to enhance your awareness and martial ability.

There are, of course, many different types of attack while using single push-hands. Try different ways, and if they work for you, then keep them.

Yin Single Push-Hands

The yin techniques are more difficult to understand than the yang because you must rely solely upon "listening energy" to know when your opponent is about to attack.

In this type of push-hands you do not have the security of P'eng to rely upon, and therefore it is a lot easier for the opponent to break through your defense. However, if you are able to learn yin push-hands, then you will come a little closer to the true meaning of taijiquan.

Figure 158

Instead of using P'eng to ward off the attack, AA will now "go in at the waist" and turn his wrist up as he brings the attack right in and out to his side. The attacker should feel as if he is attacking a bag of air (fig. 158).

After AA has defeated BB's attack, he should re-attack, and now BB should "go in at the waist" to use a yin technique, etc. When this technique is performed correctly, the wrists draw a figure eight as the two people shift forward and back.

There are many combinations that you will discover for yourself in single push-hands, but remember to stick to the basic rules: keep your wrist in your center and push with the whole body.

DOUBLE PUSH-HANDS

Double push-hands is probably the most interesting part of your taijiquan training, as this is where all of your basics are tested. Here we practice the "four cardinal directions" by performing the four attack and defense maneuvers: P'eng, Lu, Chee, and Arn.

Much has been said of the different energies used in taijiquan, and this is where you will experience them. I do not believe in filling my students' heads with a lot of esoteric jargon, preferring that they learn by experiencing it all for themselves. Only when you learn in this way will taijiquan be truly yours.

P'eng and Lu

AA and BB stand opposite each other as for single push-hands. AA holds his arms across his stomach with the right arm on top (fig. 159), while BB places both of his palms onto AA's forearms.

BB starts to push forward onto AA's arms toward the center. AA turns to his left slightly and uses P'eng to buffer the attack. At the same time AA's left wrist moves under BB's right forearm (fig. 160).

Figure 159

Figure 160

Figure 161

AA starts to turn to his right and sit all the way back onto his left leg, waits until his right wrist is to the right of his vertical center, and lightly grabs BB's right wrist. AA then sits all the way back and pulls BB toward him using the power of his waist with his left wrist above BB's right elbow (fig. 161). As BB is being pulled forward, he goes with the direction of the force and places his left palm onto the inside of his right elbow as a defense against a strong Pull Down.

NOTE: There are two techniques used in each forward or backward movement. AA has just used P'eng and Lu, while BB has used Arn and Chee.

Neutralize and Arn
As BB attacks AA with his elbow, AA should neutralize this attack by turning his waist to his left and, because of the position of his palms, directing the power from BB over to his left. BB can easily be put off balance with this move (fig. 162).

Figure 162

Now, AA will use Arn on the left arm of BB, who will perform the same movements AA has just performed. The only difference is that BB will P'eng with his left forearm and turn first to his right and then pull down. He uses his left palm to grab AA's left wrist while his right palm is on AA's left elbow as he turns to his left and sits back (fig. 163).

As you can see, this attacking and defense is now able to continue with both partners performing P'eng, Lu, Neutralize (earth), Chee, and Arn.

This is the very basic double push-hands and should be practiced on both sides.

Figure 163

Changing Directions
There are two ways to change direction. As AA is being pulled down he can, upon being pushed by BB, lift his left arm to P'eng instead of bringing the attack back onto his right arm (fig. 164).

Figure 164

Figure 165

AA now pulls down onto his left side, as in Figure 165.

The circling continues with each player performing the movements on the opposite sides from where they started.

The other way is for BB to initiate the change by making AA lift his left arm instead of his right. To do this, BB should attack with a left palm strike to AA's face after he has pulled AA backward. AA will lift his left wrist to ward off this attack and so will be forced to change direction (fig. 166).

Figure 166

Moving

Once both partners have achieved a basic proficiency, you are now able to start to move around as you perform all of these movements. AA might take a step forward as he uses Chee, forcing BB to take a step backward in defense. Or BB might take a step backward as he uses Pull Down, which would cause AA to take a step forward.

The important point is to keep the techniques going without breaks as you move around.

An important yielding technique while moving is as follows: BB might attack AA with a strong push and step through. Instead of taking a step backward, AA might step to his side as in Figure 167 and attack from the side with press (fig. 168).

Figure 167

Figure 168

Figure 169

Supplementary Push-Hands Attacks and Defense

There are many different attacking and defensive techniques you will think of while practicing push-hands. However, be sure that they work and are not too complicated. Usually you will invent some technique, and a year later it might not work as well (or at all) because of the increase in skills of one or both partners. For example, BB might attack with a strong press, and AA would simply open up both palms under BB's palms to throw him off balance (fig. 169).

From this point AA can grab both BB's arms and, using the power of his waist, throw BB to the rear, as in Figure 170.

Figure 170

Conversely, AA might use Arn in defense, as in Figure 171.

If BB grabs both of AA's elbows and attempts to lock AA in with a push as in Figure 172, AA should use his free palm to grab BB's opposite arm and throw him to the rear (fig. 173).

Figure 171

Figure 172

Figure 173

Martial Push-Hands

Push-hands can be used to teach balance, centeredness, and timing, or it can be used to teach simple blocking and attacking techniques. I have just covered the basics for the former.

For the martial application, all the players have to do is to throw different attacking techniques at the appropriate time. For instance, AA might hold BB's palm and attack his face (fig. 174)

BB would have to block this as best he could. These attacks can be used from anywhere in the practice, and the appropriate defense must be used. Once each player is well versed in both types of push-hands, the two can be combined to form an excellent training method with all kinds of practical applications, from the martial arts to helping with our daily lives.

Figure 174

PUSHING-FEET

As push-hands develops strong defensive and attacking arm and hand techniques, so pushing-feet develops the legs and feet.

The only way you will be able to keep your balance while performing this exercise is to keep your center lowered, physically and mentally. If you feel yourself going off-balance, don't struggle to keep your balance; be truthful with your-self—stop, change legs, and start again on the other side.

Begin as for single push-hands with the wrists touching. Now each player raises his right (or left) leg and joins the feet at the Achilles tendon (fig. 175).

Your feet must circle in the same direction as your hands. So if you have your right foot up, the direction is counter-clockwise. As the circling continues, AA will try and kick to BB's leg, and BB will in turn block with his ankle (fig. 176).

Once you have the foot-work under control, you may now try to attack with your palms. You may do this either simultaneously as you kick or

Figure 175

Figure 176

Figure 177

Figure 178

just circle your foot as you attack with the palm. The important point is to sink and keep your balance. Do not lean your weight onto your partner.

Other Kicking Techniques

While performing pushing-feet, you can also use different leg attacks. Your partner must block these using his legs. For instance, AA might attack with a roundhouse kick, which BB blocks using a leg, as in Figure 177.

Or AA might attack using a straight kick, which is also blocked using the leg, only this time BB attacks with his blocking foot (fig. 178).

The wrists must remain in contact at all times, even when you are attacking with your feet.

DA-LU (THE GREAT REPULSE)

Da-lu is an advanced form of push hands. In push-hands, we learn to use the four cardinal points, while in da-lu we use the four corner directions.

As with push-hands, we use

P'eng, Lu, Chee, and Arn, but we also make use of four other techniques: T'sai (pull abruptly); Leih (split); T'sou (elbow), and Kao (shoulder).

When people speak of the 13 postures (as mentioned in the taiji classics), they mean all of the above, plus the four techniques from push-hands, plus the five directions of

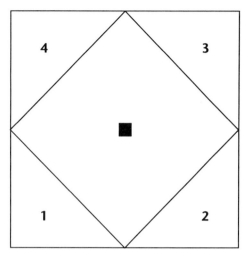

Figure 179

Step Forward (metal), Step Backward (wood), Look Left (water), Gaze Right (fire), and Central Equilibrium (earth). We also use two extra techniques, Arm Twist and Bend Backward.

Although you will be able to work out many more attacking and defensive techniques, these are the basics.

A square like the one in Figure 179 can be drawn on the floor, as this is an invaluable training aid

I have taken the photos at the best possible angle to show the technique, so look at the square in each photo to determine which corner you should be working in.

In Figure 180, AA and BB

Figure 180

Figure 181

stand opposite each other on the square as shown. AA takes a right step forward and attacks BB with a right palm strike. BB takes a left step backward and wards off with his right arm.

BB has stepped onto the diagonal of the no. 1 corner. BB now takes another step with his right foot and places it onto the same diagonal. He grabs AA's right wrist with his right palm and pulls AA forward as his weight goes onto his right leg. AA should take another step with his left foot to the center of the circle so that his feet are parallel to BB's feet (fig. 181).

To counter BB's attack, AA should now step diagonally with his right foot, placing it between BB's feet and attack with right shoulder to BB's chest, as in Figure 182.

Figure 182

To avoid being struck in his chest, BB will change his weight onto his left foot (this will cause AA's strike to miss). As he does this he strikes to AA's face with his right palm, blocks AA's right elbow with his left palm and takes a step with his right foot, placing it near AA's right foot (fig. 183).

NOTE: There are three steps in attack and only two in defense. The step that BB has just taken is his first in attack in this new sequence.

To avoid being struck, AA now steps onto the no. 2 diagonal with his left foot and uses P'eng to ward off the attack (fig. 184).

Figure 183

Figure 184

Figure 185

AA now grabs BB's right wrist with his right palm and takes another step onto the diagonal with his right foot and pulls BB backward as BB has just done to him. BB should take his second step with his left foot to the center of the square so that his feet are parallel to AA's (fig. 185).

BB now steps in with his right foot, placing it between AA's feet, and attacks with his shoulder, as in Figure 186.

Figure 186

You can see that the whole process of attack and defense has now been reversed. From here it is a simple matter of repeating these steps so that BB now steps into the no. 3 corner and pulls downward as AA attacks with his right shoulder, as in Figure 187. AA now steps into the no. 4 corner and attacks with Pull Down as BB attacks with the right shoulder (fig. 188).

Now you have completed the four corners. If you keep going you will simply keep repeating these movements into the same corners.

Figure 187

Figure 188

Figure 189

Changing Direction Using Arn

If we take it from Figure 182, AA will now step between BB's feet with his left foot and use Press on BB's left arm instead of Slap (fig. 189).

BB will step backward with his right foot onto the previous diagonal and use P'eng to ward off AA's attack, as in Figure 190.

Figure 190

Then BB will step with his left foot onto that same diagonal and pull AA forward. AA, having taken a step in attack, will take another step to the center of the square with his right foot and then another one with his left foot between BB's feet to attack BB's chest with his left shoulder (fig. 191).

The direction has changed. BB can now slap AA's face with his left palm and step with his left foot, while AA will ward off with his left arm and step to the no. 4 diagonal with his right foot. AA can then pull BB down as BB advances with two more steps to attack AA's chest with his left shoulder, and so it goes on in the opposite direction.

When you use Slap to counter your partner's Shoulder, you will continue on to the next diagonal, whereas if you use Arn to change direction, you will go back onto the previous diagonal.

Once these basic movements have become second nature, you may either use Slap or Shoulder at will. This will increase your awareness greatly, along with your ability to move with an attacker to gain the upper hand.

There are many more attack-

Figure 191

Figure 192

Figure 193

Figure 194

ing and defensive movements that you will be able to put into this practice. For instance, you could use Bend Backward as your opponent comes in with a Shoulder (fig. 192).

Conversely, you could use Arm Twist instead of Pull Down (fig. 193).

A FINAL TRAINING METHOD

Two players stand opposite each other; one is the attacker (BB), and the other is the defender (AA).

BB strikes to AA's face with a right hook punch. AA should swivel both of his toes 45 degrees to his left and block the attack with his left palm as he simultaneously attacks BB's face with his right palm (fig. 194).

The block should not be forced but should circle naturally with the momentum of the body as it turns. The right palm should also move in harmony with the body as it turns. You should be practice this on both sides until you can repel an attacker on any side at any time.

From the last maneuver, the attacker might punch low to the right lower rib area of AA. AA should swivel his body to his right and, as he does, swing his left forearm downward to his right to block the attack. As in Figure 195, AA places his right palm on the top of his own left forearm to prevent the attack from slipping upward.

From this position, AA can either just wait until the next attack or counter by grabbing BB's left wrist, stepping forward with his left foot, and attacking BB's face with his left backfist, as in Figure 196.

Figure 195

This also happens on the other side. Now your attacker is able to attack high or low on either side at any time, and you must be able to block and counterattack simultaneously. The lower block can also be used against kicks.

CONCLUSION

Don't get into the old "You can't push *me* over" routine, because there is always someone bigger and stronger. Learn to yield to an attack and use the larger opponent's

Figure 196

energy against him. Move out of the way of a heavy attack, preferably to the closed side, but if this is impossible then make the most of your evasive ability.

Learn to attack from anywhere at any time. If you are attacked during push-hands practice, always follow up with an attack after your defensive maneuver or make your defensive maneuver your attack.

If your arm is pulled with great force and you are unable to break the hold, relax your weight and go with the force, redirecting it back into the opponent. The stronger your opponent's attack, the stronger your response will be.

Remember to practice push-hands and the other training methods as a martial art and not for the sake of doing push-hands.

Keep in mind that if your own technique works against someone who is, perhaps, at the same level as you, it may not work against someone more experienced.

chapter four

When we look at a taiji exponent who is considered a master of the art, we will notice that many of his movements are not quite the same as those we have been taught. Sometimes, for instance, when I give workshops for my schools worldwide, some students are worried that what they have learned is not exactly the same as what I am doing.

This is because I am doing taiji at the fourth, or *hao ch'uan* ("loose boxing") level, whereas the students are doing it at one of the other three levels of skill/experience: beginning level, where we learn each of the movements in block form—the simplest way to teach beginners; level 2, where we begin to connect the blocks without stopping; or level 3, where we learn about opening and closing or yin and yang.

Level 4, hao ch'uan, is where most of the ends of the movements have a fa-jing, or explosive shake.

There are certain postures that are totally different at the highest level, and at this advanced stage we are able to use the "opening and closing" movements to make the greatest use of our internal energy. Every posture has an open/yin and a closed/yang part.

In addition, in keeping with the double-fish taiji symbol, there is also some yang within yin and vice-versa. Also, the

ADVANCED
CONCEPTS:
THE
FOUR
LEVELS
OF TAIJI

whole form continues like a sine wave, opening at the beginning, closing up at the postures known as Hit Tiger at Left and Hit Tiger at Right, then opening up again from Fair Lady Works the Shuttles to the end of the form. This is when it is performed on the right-hand side. (When the form is done starting on the left-hand side as a mirror-image exercise, the "opening and closing" reverses.)

It is important to remember that developing our grasp of the internal cannot be forced, although it can be encouraged. Perhaps one of the keys to going from level to level over the years is being able to see someone, whether in person or on video, do taiji at levels that are greater than our own.

To be able to work at developing something, we first have to be aware that it exists! For example, until I learn about the existence of "opening and closing" and then see someone perform such intricate movements while doing form, it is impossible to try to copy it. To further complicate matters, I won't be able to "see" the movements unless I have already attained a certain level—even if I am told that such movements do exist.

Exceptional students may be able to make quantum leaps of experiential, as opposed to theoretical, understanding, but most of us will have to learn step-by-step, year-by-year.

Subtle Energy Release in the Yang Ch'eng-fu Form

The classics tell us that one of the most important things in our practice is to remember the distinction between yin and yang and the changes in between. We learn to build up yang energy by performing a yin movement and release it using a yang movement, which, in turn, creates a potential yin energy.

When asked what was the most important thing in all of taijiquan, Fu Zhongwen (Yang Ch'eng-fu's nephew) told me that it was this distinction.

However, being told this and learning *how* to do it are two very different matters. So what do we do when the Chinese translation doesn't give us much in the way of technical detail? Anyone can know when he or she is weighted on one foot and empty on the other, but differentiating between yin and yang goes far beyond this particular physical difference!

We must also learn to distinguish between yin and yang in the mind, and this is the most important aspect of our training. However, only the practitioner can know when these minute changes in the mind occur. When they do, then the whole physical form will change to incorporate, for example, a small shake here, a slight twist there. The casual observer won't be able to detect easily how the form has changed, except that it looks somehow different and more "alive."

Although forms such as those in the Chen style and the Yang Lu-ch'an style have these subtle changes, they also have the most obvious energy-release points of fa-jing. The latter are important because of the greater qi buildup derived from these forms; hence, the greater reciprocal release points.

The Yang Ch'eng-fu form does not have these overt fa-jing release points. Instead, it relies upon even more subtle internal fa-jing movements, which manifest themselves physically as minute movements of the wrist or waist.

Once we are able to do the Yang Ch'eng-fu form so well that the mind is not continually thinking about what to do next, we are able to concentrate on "no-mind" during our practice—or, should I say, we concentrate on not concentrating on no-mind!

When the conscious mind does not think about what we are doing, the brain is able to go into what is called an alpha state. This is when we are not awake or asleep; it's that stage when we are just dropping off to sleep but not quite. So we begin the form, and the next thing the conscious brain knows is that we are finishing.

This is the point when taijiquan becomes your own and not the property of your teacher. It becomes your own creation with minuscule movements that only your body shape will be able to perform, movements that will be different from anyone else's form but still keep to the original basic pattern you were taught.

Achieving no-mind is not just learning to eliminate "mental

chatter" but also creating continuous movement in the mind and body, which will then begin to show physically, with every part of you—right down to the smallest part of your body—in a state of unending action.

People who are naturally talented physically make mistakes when they try to force their body movement to be continuous from outside. For instance, a dancer or athlete will quickly exhibit the external appearance of continuous bodily movement for the posture of Brush Knee, Twist Step. However, to be a true internal movement, this flow must happen from the inside and not be forced prematurely.

The true test of internal movement is to watch the wrists. Were they flexed all the way to the striking position? This would indicate a noninternal energy release, as the body has changed physically and a push has occurred but there has not been a potential difference in the wrist. More correctly, when the internal manifests itself, the wrist will first build up with potential energy by becoming relaxed and alive.

"Relaxed and alive" means that the wrist is not totally dropped down but rather is still alive with a small portion of yang energy as dictated to us by the yin/yang symbol. Now, as the wrist attacks, keeping to the center of the body and moved by the action of the body turning to the front, it slowly flexes slightly until it has released its built-up potential energy upon impact.

The wrist is not, however, fully flexed, as this indicates no presence of yin energy and is wrong. Every movement you make must have this energy release, be it ever so small. For example, in doing the posture of Chee, one must squeeze the elbows in slightly to allow for the internal fa-jing. When P'eng is performed, the wrist is not fully bent from the beginning but rather slowly flexes during the movement. In the posture of Lift Hands you should not bring the palms too close together, as this indicates a fully discharged state. The palms should be kept apart as if you are trying to squeeze something that will not squeeze.

Shoulder Stroke is always a difficult posture to understand. Although there is only a slight turning of the waist and the power all seems to come from the rear leg, you should notice the right wrist. As you shift onto your forward leg, the wrist will also slowly bend under so that at the end it is almost fully flexed. If you were to perform this at full power and speed, of course, this wrist movement is explosive, thus sending the energy to the shoulder.

Stork Spreads Wings is another posture that seems to have only physical movement, but look at any person who has been practicing taiji correctly for many years, and you will see that there is a slight "shake" upon execution of this posture.

Brush Knee, Twist Step also has this slight shake at the end of the movement, with the waist turning slightly in the opposite direction of the strike. This seems contradictory to the flow, but when the movement is performed at full power and speed, the reason for the twist becomes evident: to provide the counter-movement to gain torque and fa-jing.

Potential Energy

We should look at taijiquan as a continual building up and releasing of potential energy, i.e., the potential energy changes state into a usable form. When we relax the wrist, lifting it slightly, this indicates a buildup of potential energy. When we flex the wrist slightly, this signals the change of state into a usable form of energy.

Combine this with the correct breath and centered movement, and we have the perfect energy transference mechanism. After all, what are we doing in either the healing or the fighting art but simply causing energy changes to happen in our own and others' bodies, even if it is as obvious as a slap in the mouth?

Even in such a crude instance, we have built up energy with the movement just before the attack and changed that potential energy into attacking energy when we made contact. In healing, we are using an extremely subtle energy change in placing our palms onto someone's body, and with minute physical and internal changes in yin and yang energy, we are able to send a constant energy flow into that part of the body.

Aside from form practice, you can use the following exercise as a means of experiencing what taijiquan is really about in the long-term.

Set aside one hour a day when you perform your mundane tasks to keep the taijiquan principles in mind—or, rather, not in mind!

You should begin by just standing for a few moments, allowing your whole body to "collapse" into the backbone, bending slightly at the knees. Be rid of all physical thought and allow your body to be dictated to by your inner mind. Think about what is under your feet; place your mind on this area. Change your weight and try to feel the slight changes that occur. Slowly pick up one foot and maintain perfect balance as you begin to walk, placing your foot down slowly and carefully so that no weight is plonked onto it, but rather slowly transferred onto it.

Allow your arms to do what the movement dictates as you perform your daily "things." You will at first only be able to do this at a slow pace, and you will prefer to do it indoors away from onlookers because you will feel silly. After some time you will be able to move more quickly while still keeping this balance of movement and transference of energy.

Eventually, you will be able to keep the entire day in balance, and your whole life will be enhanced through "being" taijiquan from moment to moment as opposed to "doing" taijiquan for a half-hour a day.

chapter five

As in many aspects of taijiquan, there is an apparent contradiction inherent in learning the martial applications for the various postures that make up the long form: if you don't understand the individual techniques, your skill cannot become internal; however, if you concentrate too narrowly on techniques, your skill cannot become internal!

Sadly for the state of taiji as a method of self-defense, the majority of modern practitioners are never exposed to even the most basic function of the postures contained in the forms. They remain content to "go through the motions" while doing solo form. In fact, most of the beginners I teach don't even know that taiji is a martial art when they start classes!

Conversely, a minority of practitioners go to obsessive lengths to practice applications—building a vast arsenal of techniques, some of which are well-honed at a basic level while others are poorly understood.

However, it is not enough to learn push-hands and build a vast arsenal of individual techniques. Self-defense situations don't allow you the time to analyze what's being thrown at you so that you can mentally sort through the possible responses to pick the one that seems appropriate.

You either respond intuitively and immediately to an attack or "lose face" in

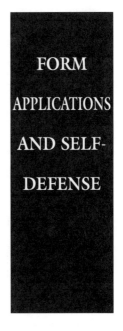

FORM APPLICATIONS AND SELF-DEFENSE

ways that go beyond the original meaning of that Chinese expression!

The true value of the form applications lies somewhere between the two extremes. It is essential that each student have an understanding of what he or she is doing martially at any given point in the form. Without the active use of the mind, qi cannot move freely, and you reduce your practice to a low-level form of exercise or external kung-fu.

There are also basic and more advanced applications for each posture, and as your skill and understanding deepen, so should your appreciation of the patterns of movement and lines of energy inherent in any martial exchange.

It is obviously beneficial to practice applications with a partner periodically to sharpen your mental and physical "feel" for what you are doing when you practice form. However, it is not necessary to "get good" at doing these techniques, as real self-defense skills are honed by internalizing a few techniques that are particularly suited to your build and temperament and by practicing the applications forms and related training methods.

With this caveat in mind, I have included basic applications of selected postures in this chapter to aid your own exploration of what the postures can mean martially. Experiment with partners, discard what doesn't work for you, and keep what does!

FORM APPLICATIONS

Quite often the applications will vary in detail slightly from what you do when practicing solo. This is partly because having a partner always introduces random variables that force you to modify what you do "in theory" when faced with a martial "reality." It is also partly because the slow form was consciously altered at the turn of the century when taiji started being taught to the general public, as opposed to relatives and friends of the instructors only. This was done to make it difficult for the casual observer to learn the martial secrets of the Yang style.

NOTE: Please keep in mind the limitations inherent in trying to demonstrate with still photography techniques whose effectiveness depends on movement. Photos can only show the end of each posture, and it is really the actions that lead to the final moment that are important in taiji. I would like to thank Sean Kelly and Marc Sequin, two of my senior students, for posing in the photos with me.

Beginning

Your arms whip upward as you rock the body forward into the attacker's grabbing movements (fig. 197).

As you rock back slightly and shift your center of balance downward, your hands jerk the attacker's arms down to cause whiplash in his neck and also pull his face into your forehead (fig. 198).

Figure 197

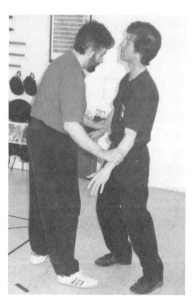

Figure 198

Figure 199

Figure 200

Block Across the Right

The attacker throws a low roundhouse punch with his left to your right side. As in Figure 199, you swivel on the heels and bump the attacking arm with the left wrist while slamming down on top of the attacking wrist with the heel of your right palm.

Single Ward-Off

After the previous action, you "bounce" forward, your left foot touches down, then you jerk the attacking hand downward to upset your attacker's equilibrium and cause minor whiplash while striking to the side of his face with a backfist (fig. 200).

Double P'eng

This application is a little more advanced and requires good timing. Your attacker advances and throws a right high punch. As in Figure 201, you immediately move forward and bump his arm slightly off-target while simultaneously striking his throat with your right P'eng while your left palm scrapes up his attacking arm to upset his equilibrium and "rub against the grain" of the qi flow in his arm.

Figure 201

Pull Down

Your attacker strikes low with the right hand. You slam the heel of your left palm and the back of your right hand down onto the attacking arm to damage it (fig. 202). Shifting the weight back as you do so puts all of your body weight into such a strike and pulls the attacker downward and to one side of you.

Figure 202

Figure 203

Squeeze

Taking advantage of the previous posture to set up your next move, you shift forward and execute Squeeze as a concussive strike against the attacker's upper arm to deaden it (fig. 203). He should already be twisted off balance to your advantage.

Press Forward

As a follow-up to the previous posture, shift forward and press forward and up to trap his left arm across his chest as you uproot him (fig. 204).

Figure 204

Fishes in Eight

Intercepting a high punch with the left hand as shown in Figure 205, you jerk the attacker's wrist, pulling him around to your rear, and simultaneously strike him in the side with the right elbow.

As an immediate follow-up to this while he is still off balance, you immediately sweep your right hand into his throat while your left palm shocks up his left arm (fig. 206).

Figure 205

Figure 206

Figure 207

Single Whip

Your right hand hooks to intercept a straight punch and sweep it to one side and back as you turn slightly to your right and shift your weight back slightly (fig. 207).

You use that circling momentum to shift slightly forward to strike in a *downward* fashion with the knuckles of the hooked hand. Done properly, this will upset the attacker's balance to prevent him from easily stopping your countermove (fig. 208).

Figure 208

Brush Knee, Twist Step

Your rising knee turns inward slightly to block a low kick, as in Figure 209. Following this, you immediately slam the heel of your left palm onto the attacking leg and then shift forward to press your attacker further off balance as you attack his solar plexus with a right palm strike (fig. 210).

Figure 209

Figure 210

Figure 211

"False Step" and Hands Strum the Lute

Your attacker blocks and grabs your right wrist with his right hand. Using this to your advantage, you lift and drop your rear foot to put all of your body weight into pulling him forward and off balance (fig. 211).

As your foot drops, you shift back onto your rear leg, which jerks his right arm straight, making it more vulnerable to the strike you direct into his right elbow with your left palm (fig. 212).

Figure 212

Step Up, Deflect, Parry and Punch

In response to your attacker grabbing your left wrist with his left hand, you do a weighted turn to the left, which pulls him off balance as your right fist strikes his right arm (fig. 213).

Using the rising momentum of this, you circle the right fist to block a strike from his other hand and kick him in the shin with the inside of the right foot (fig. 214).

Figure 213

Figure 214

Figure 215

Step forward with the left leg as the attacker continues with a right-hand punch, which you parry and follow with a right-hand punch of your own under the attacking arm into his side (fig. 215).

Fist under Elbow

Turning, you almost simultaneously parry with the right hand while striking to the throat with the left fingers. The left foot could kick the attacker's shin, as it is empty of weight (fig. 216).

Figure 216

Repulse Monkey

Your right hand pumps downward into the attacker's face as you use the back of the left hand to strike and stop the low punch thrown at you (fig. 217).

Golden Needle at the Sea Bottom

Modifying the posture from form, you snake the edge of your captive hand over the attacker's grip and hold his fingers with your other hand to snap him to his knees with the pressure exerted on the wrist (fig. 218).

Figure 217

Figure 218

Figure 219

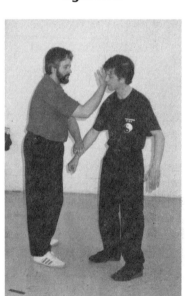

Figure 220

Fan through the Back

If he tries to release his hand or pull backward, regrip his wrist with your right hand and, rising, take a step and thrust under his armpit with your left hand (fig. 219).

Wave Hands Like Clouds

One hand pushes down to deflect an attacking arm while the other rotates up and forward to strike the attacker's face (fig. 220).

High Pat the Horse

The back of the left hand deflects a punch downward while the right hand simultaneously shoots forward to strike the attacker's face, as in Figure 221. Shifting the weight back as you do so adds body momentum to the technique.

Draw the Bow

Using your right palm, you deflect a straight punch while stepping diagonally to your left to move your body out of the way of the initial attack. As in Figure 222, your left palm arcs across from right to left to strike the attacker's temple.

Figure 221

Figure 222

Figure 223

Figure 224

Separation of Left Leg

Deflect the attacking arm with the crossed wrists and immediately jerk the wrist with one hand while striking the attacker's face with the lead hand. Then kick the attacker's lead leg, just below the knee on the side with a circling kick, using the edge of the foot to strike (fig. 223).

Punch the Triple Warmer Points

As the attacker punches, do a weighted turn of the right leg and use the palm of the left hand to deflect the attack down and to the side. Stepping through and grabbing the wrist of the arm you just struck, pull the attacker off balance while punching the upper arm to make that limb "go dead" by affecting certain points (fig. 224).

Hit Tiger Right

As the attacker strikes low, sweep the right arm down to strike the attacking limb (Figure 225).

Continuing to sweep the arm out of the way with the forward momentum of your body, use a twisting punch to the attacker's head with the same arm (fig. 226). Your other arm also strikes his side or acts as a guard against retaliation.

Figure 225

Figure 226

Figure 227

Figure 228

Slanting Flying

As you step behind your attacker's lead leg, you jerk his captive hand to your side, then immediately shift forward to slam the edge of your right hand against his throat (fig. 227). This can also have the effect of upsetting him over your lead leg.

Fair Lady Works at the Shuttles

Your attacker punches and you move forward to upset his timing, get inside his lines of focus, and deflect the attack upward with the left forearm as you pump to the side with your right palm (fig. 228).

Golden Cock Stands on One Leg

Use your left arm to bump the attacking arm slightly off target while simultaneously lifting your left knee into the lower body (fig. 229).

Cross Hands to Penetrate

Your right palm strikes the attacking arm, pushing it downward so that you can step forward with the left foot and thrust your left fingertips into the attacker's throat (fig. 230).

Figure 229

Figure 230

Figure 231

Snake Creeps Down

Your attacker grabs your left hand, and you shift backward and use the momentum of squatting to pull him off balance (fig. 231).

Immediately, you shift forward and rise up to thrust the same hand into the attacker's groin, as in Figure 232.

Figure 232

Step Up to Seven Stars

By moving in suddenly, you upset the attacker's timing and strike his throat on both sides with the edges of your fists (fig. 233).

Lotus Kick

Deflect his attack to the side with both palms; this may spin him partially around, making it easier for you to kick him in the area of the kidney with the right leg that sweeps up from left to right (fig. 234).

Figure 233

Figure 234

Figure 235

Shoot the Tiger

Deflect a high attack upward with the right fist as you step into the attack at a diagonal and hammer down on the attacker's nose at the same time. Power comes from the forward shifting and the twisting of the upper torso.

SELF-DEFENSE

Even when taken at a basic level of martial competence, the applications shown all share a few things in common.

Reduced to their essence, these methods encompass the following: 1) get out of the way of the incoming force or move forward to counterattack at the same time; 2) upset the attacker's balance just before counterstriking to make it harder for him to defend; 3) move your body whenever possible to put all of your weight into your tactics; 4) strike vital points (i.e., throat), preferably almost at the same time as you defend; and 5) there are no blocks in taiji—you defend by striking to damage the attacking limb and/or upset his timing.

Harsh though such tactics may seem, sensitivity and yielding, two much talked-about keystones in taiji, must be present in them. However, these two attributes should be a means to an end, not "golden idols" in themselves.

It can be a painful lesson to learn that a tactic that works well with a partner in your class is likely to collapse if tested by someone whose martial style emphasizes committed attacks or against the adrenaline-powered swings of an attacker fueled by rage and/or alcohol and drugs.

Sadly, from my own experience with students and instructors of many styles, it is obvious that most modern taijiquan is a poor reflection of the original training.

The harsh reality of what works and what doesn't is difficult to appreciate for those modern students who are drawn initially to the Yang style by its philosophical and meditative aspects and/or its reputation as an "effortless" martial art.

Such students often have little or no experience with the more aggressive external styles and feel an unwarranted contempt for sweat and effort. The latter are as much an essential ingredient of the internal martial arts as they are for mastering *any* worthwhile discipline.

In addition, working with a variety of partners of different sizes and skill levels is essential in martial terms. When two people of different skill levels work together it can be easy for each to get an inadequate sense of how effective they would be if they were really obliged to use their skills defensively.

Furthermore, very few instructors attempt to apply the principles of their art to realistic fighting situations by having their students train, at least some of the time, against vigorous attacks by students who *know how to attack in an effective manner.*

It is very true that martial training usually makes the practitioner less likely to get into meaningless fights or be aggressive. However, lack of training is no handicap to those numerous individuals who have learned the hard way, on the streets, to take and throw a punch. In addition, drugs and alcohol can make an attacker immune to pain in a way that has to be experienced to be appreciated.

Since we are talking about basics in this book, we will lay aside the more advanced aspects of fa-jing (an explosive force generated by a spiraling shake of the body that is initiated in the waist to "get there first with the most," to paraphrase Nathan Beford Forrest, a Confederate general in the American Civil War, when he was asked to explain how he won his battles); the use of the reptile mind (that primitive part of the brain that is programmed only for the basic biological func-

Figure 236

tions of feeding, reproduction, and survival); and dim-mak (vital point striking).

At the most basic level, two essential aspects of developing self-defense skills are timing and relaxation.

Timing must be considered from the standpoint of your body's ability to generate, transmit, and deliver force at the right time to the right target. Effective timing is dependent on your perceptual sensitivity so that you can launch your attack as soon as the attacker commits his in your direction. You can't develop such sensitivity unless you're relaxed in every sense of the word!

Such well-timed counterattacks allow you to cancel out the attacking energy as you, in effect, block and strike with one action (fig. 236).

Relaxation, in martial terms, implies using only the right muscles to do the right task at hand. A stiff attack from an amateur is relatively easy to deal with if you can relax even marginally more than your opponent. However, stiffness combined with rage and/or skill is a different proposition and one not usually met when training in a classroom setting.

In addition, a well-timed movement achieves maximum effect if your supporting leg thrusts strongly into the ground and no blockage caused by tension occurs in any part of the body. The existence of such a blockage reduces the amount of force that will reach the target.

Ideally, this force acts in a wavelike manner, flowing upward from the foot and leg, being directed by the hips, passing through the shoulder, and moving down the arm to the hand. Correct timing combined with effective relaxation ensures the unbroken wavelike effect of this force with maximum impact on the target.

When this internal martial art is taught improperly, its very strength—the ability to change tactics as the circumstances demand—can easily become a liability if not balanced with the necessary commitment.

To put it simply, you have to be sure your tactic has failed before you try something else, and then you have to be willing to persevere with the new tactic until you're sure it has failed.

You often see the effect of a lack of commitment when two reasonably well-matched taiji students practice together. Such training often settles into an exchange of constantly aborted tactics. One person will attack, feel his opponent start to neutralize the attack, and switch to another tactic *before there is really a need to do so.* The other will respond in a similar manner so that neither really attempts to succeed with a particular technique.

No one, no matter what his skill level, knows how he will react until he is faced with real danger. The expert may freeze and get injured by the wildest swing; the relative beginner may instantly defuse the situation with a few calm words or a simple tactic.

Sadly, if you want to maximize your self-defense potential, you have to train accordingly—by practicing with power against power—at least some of the time. In combat terms, it is essential that you not "freeze," either physically or emotionally, if struck or suddenly forced to fight. You must respond with effective tactics *immediately.*

Survival usually rests with those who blend offensive and defensive tactics and don't just hope to stumble upon a suitable tactic by being totally on the defensive. I find it difficult to be patient with taiji students and instructors who obviously believe their own stories about being able to project qi at an attacker or of not needing to learn combat skills because they know how to stick and neutralize.

When you push or strike such people while training, they

become annoyed and accuse you of using too much muscle. They might be better off asking themselves why the use of force succeeded!

Fear

Many beginners are attracted to the martial arts partly because they feel at risk in some way in their daily lives. This may be because they or someone they know has been victimized at some time or because they are afraid of it happening.

Unfortunately, this same motivation, fear, is a complex factor in whether or not these individuals might be able to use the skills they develop to defend themselves or their loved ones effectively.

Fear (and its accompanying adrenaline rush) can bring unexpected vigor to your response if you are attacked and lack the time to let your nerves get the better of you. Or it can leave you completely open to the slowest and stupidest of attacks.

Conversely, the martially skilled person who is still struggling emotionally to overcome fears may find it difficult to avoid overreacting with combat skills that should be reserved for life-and-death situations. Crushing a windpipe because someone bigger and uglier than you shoved your shoulders a few times in a crowded bar is a sad expression of your training. In addition, the resulting arrest for excessive force and/or lawsuit from the victim's family will only give you further reason to regret your lack of control.

Of course, it's easy for an armchair expert (or even an experienced martial arts instructor like myself) to generalize about how you should react against a real aggressor. None of us know how we will act until we are thrust into such a situation, and each situation will be different.

However, it is equally true that if you can't make your martial skills work against an unrehearsed and committed attack from your instructor or fellow student, then you probably don't have much hope of successfully defending yourself against a real attacker. It is easy to talk about being calm in the face of danger when you are in a classroom setting; it's much harder to achieve this state when someone larger than you is screaming in your face while being goaded on by his friends.

This is particularly true if you do an internal martial art that has dispensed with hard, skilled, and determined attacks as a part of its training curriculum. Sadly, this is the case in the majority of such schools where pious statements about "avoiding the use of force" and "neutralizing and yielding overcoming brute strength" have replaced combat common sense.

Most of the techniques and skills that you will practice in your taiji are useful ways of learning self-discipline, of developing specific physical attributes and expressing yourself martially according to your particular style. Such training brings physical and emotional insights and, with enough time and hard-work, should produce combat skills that *might* serve you well against an aggressive *amateur*.

The key word here is "amateur," and this is where most martial arts training fails to come to terms with reality. It's not enough to train to defend yourself against someone like yourself, i.e., a nice person. Rather, in terms of self-defense skills, as opposed to martial skills, you have to train with the worst possible scenario in mind.

I have seen a 140-pound man who was drunk and enraged to the point of insanity fight his way through a half-dozen men trying to restrain him, despite his having been hit in the head several times with a chair. It's going to be a challenge to defend yourself against someone similar by "yielding with softness to his aggression."

Even in a class setting, it has been my experience that most students, no matter how skilled and experienced, have trouble actually stopping a sudden, aggressive attack from me, even when they know that I'm not really going to hurt them. Would it be different if they were faced by a real aggressor, either an experienced brawler or someone just big and enraged?

It's hard to know, but I can assure you of one thing—if you can't keep your instructor from getting his hands around your throat while ramming you into a wall, your chances of doing it to someone mean and angry are awfully small!

At least some of the time in your training, you have to prac-

Figure 237

Figure 238

tice applying your skills against someone who rushes in, doesn't care whether he gets hit anywhere except for vital points, and keeps coming until he has you against the wall or on the floor.

Such training has only a two requirements: a heavily padded and skillful "aggressor" who attacks suddenly and/or violently (fig. 237) and won't stop advancing unless hit somewhere vital (fig. 238), and students willing to put their martial "egos" at risk.

Remaining calm under pressure is essential in martial terms but is very difficult to do. The "no mind" of Taoism and Zen Buddhism is, I think, a more philosophically acceptable expression of the reptile mind mentioned earlier.

In combat terms, both have the same result—removing the effects of moral training from our actions. The aggressor is no longer another human being with a family and a personality both good and bad; he or she is reduced to being a dangerous threat that must be neutralized as quickly and as efficiently as possible without contemplation of ethics or consequences.

To the reptile mind, the intrusion of sudden movement can signal only "do I eat this?" or "will it eat me?"; if it is the latter, "do I run?" or "do I attack?" In self-defense terms, running away (i.e., avoiding trouble by removing yourself from a potentially dangerous scenario) is always best if it can be done safely. Unfortunately, you rarely can do this safely, as most real assaults are sudden and at close-range.

In many ways, attacking with spontaneous movements powered by the reptile/no mind is the only real option against a committed or crazy aggressor, as opposed to relying on a passive defense or specific techniques.

However, even at a basic level of skill, your fear must energize your self-defense skills, not overwhelm them. Your internal martial training should make you neither an easy victim nor a paranoid powder keg waiting to explode.

Real violence springs seemingly out of nowhere, usually when you least expect it. The first one or two effective techniques usually decide who is the victim and who is the victor. And you can't always avoid violence by minding your own business.

If you're not used to getting hit, the first blow will probably hurt/shock you enough to leave you open to subsequent blows from an enraged drunk or experienced attacker.

Unlike in the movies, where fights go on for what seems like hours, real violence tends to start and be over before you can analyze what is happening. Kicks are rarely used unless with an element of surprise or to finish someone who has been knocked down.

It is easy to get carried away with feelings of spiritual or tactical superiority when doing a martial art like taijiquan. This is especially true if you only train in push-hands or limit your sparring to no contact.

However, the "good guys" don't always win in real life, and moral superiority is small consolation for a beating that leaves you (or a loved one) psychologically or physically maimed.

There are many stories about the old Chinese master who passively allows himself to be beaten by a gang of laughing ruffians. When they leave, he gets up as if nothing has happened, while, over the following days, the ruffians are all incapacitated by injuries caused by the beating they thought they were giving to their victim.

Having had the experience of striking a modern-day master or two with stiff force, only to have it rebound painfully into my limbs, I will admit that there may well be something in such old tales. However, most of us aren't capable of such marvelous demonstrations of passive resistance!

If you train in an internal martial art for meditative or health reasons only, that's fine, but please don't think that the benefits you find through solo slow form and qigong will somehow bring salvation if you're ever attacked.

No one, no matter what his skill level, knows how he will react until faced with real danger. The expert may freeze and get injured by the wildest swing; the relative beginner may instantly defuse the situation with a few calm words or a simple tactic.

No martial training can guarantee that you will be able to defend yourself successfully against *any* aggressor. However, such training should give you a "fighting chance." Properly taught and practiced, taijiquan is an insurance policy that also pays dividends in the form of good physical, emotional, and spiritual health.

TRAINING DURATION AND INTENSITY

I once heard someone say, "Writing is easy! All you have to do is stare at the paper until beads of sweat form on your forehead!" Training in an internal martial art is certainly comparable.

With proper instruction and ongoing practice, *eventually* your practice will no longer rely on the conscious mind and physical strength. At this point in your development of the forms and methods of the internal arts, you can continue to refine your practice until the day you die—ideally while training!

The same cannot be said of external stylists. With few exceptions, their skills either wither with age or they stumble upon a "semi-internal" way of doing things. Sadly, most just wither. For example, I recently saw a local middle-aged Shao-lin instructor demonstrate his forms, and it was more than a little sad to see someone my age huffing and puffing his way stiffly through such movements.

By contrast, many instructors of the internal styles are *entering* their martial prime at age 40. The average older internal practitioner may have to modify the intensity of each session or substitute a slow form for a fast or slow/fast form as he enters his 50s or 60s but has no legitimate age-related reason to stop completely. I know a Wu-style taiji instructor who is 70, and he still trains for an hour every day and teaches several times a week.

Such continuity is, of course, only possible if you train in a style that uses sound body mechanics. Forms that allow the knees to rotate out of alignment may go unnoticed when you're a fit 25-year-old but, in the long-run, destroy your joints by the time you turn 40.

Aside from using proper body mechanics in your internal training, it is also important to practice moderately and on an ongoing basis. Stop all activity/training for a few months or years when you are past 40, for example, and it will be more difficult to resume your practice *safely*, especially if you are practicing vigorous forms, and these are the ones that are the most beneficial to your overall health.

It is also true that it is more difficult to begin training in a vigorous form of taiji if you are past 35. You should check with your doctor and pace yourself according to your level of fitness.

The length of each of your training sessions and their frequency in your schedule are dependent on a number of variables: your own interest, physical ability, and time constraints, as well as what your instructor recommends.

For example, two or three hours of instruction per week can be sufficient if it is bolstered by daily solo practice. It is certainly true that few modern teachers, much less their students, practice with the intensity that the old masters brought to their training. Of course, in "those days" the latter had to be skilled at a variety of methods and weapons, as they never knew when they would be challenged by a rival and, again, had to train at a level of intensity that is alien to most of us.

When I read about a taiji master who routinely goes through his long form 10 to 20 times a day or who practices four to five hours in the evening after a full day of work, I find it hard to believe that anyone is capable of such intensity or interest.

These days, few of us with families or occupations can match such training regimes, but it remains true that regular practice is essential to making progress—especially if your interest goes beyond doing form.

I find it difficult to be patient with the middle-aged taiji practitioners and instructors I meet who obviously believe that doing a short form once a day somehow makes them "internally" superior to a young hard-stylist who practices one or two hours a day.

While on the subject of length of form, and at the risk of offending many, I have come to believe that people, except absolute beginners, are wasting their time learning and practicing any of the *modern short/modified* forms. If I have one recommendation for the serious student of taiji, it is to learn and practice a competent, traditional long form or don't bother!

Earlier, Erle discussed the optimal way of practicing form, and once a day should be the bare minimum if you hope to see any real self-healing benefits from the practice of long form.

In martial terms, you also should regularly practice a few selected techniques at a fast/fa-jing pace to supplement your slow form practice. Pick one or two combinations that you particularly like and do well, and do as many repetitions as you can manage without exhausting yourself. These techniques should be practiced while striking the air, pads or heavy bags, and against a partner.

You are much better off with one or two powerful, internalized techniques (especially if they are "driven" by fa-jing) rather than dozens that you have to think about before you can do them.

Even though on a functional level the leg techniques in the internal arts are all aimed low, it is important to practice them (in the forms only) as high as you can manage for the exercise value. Just be careful to not try to kick higher than your joints are ready for.

The Taoistic basis of the internal arts should lead us to understand that the self-healing and combat skills are gained gradually through moderate and balanced training. An internal martial art is difficult to cultivate through either obsessive or lackadaisical training.

The obsessive younger student may quickly develop basic martial skills but destroy his emotional/spiritual sense of balance; the older obsessive student may train too hard initially and burn himself out on a physical or emotional level. By contrast, the lackadaisical student trains only when the mood takes him and then overinflates the value of such training.

On a pragmatic level, if you never sweat or ache as a result of your training, then you're probably not doing enough to make real progress. If you ache all the time and feel exhausted after training, then you're probably overdoing it.

Without laboring the point, serious students of an internal art must search out the best available versions of their art and practice them moderately and regularly to make progress. Once gained, internal martial skills are there for life and need not be practiced as much to remain useful.

If you are training in fast or fa-jing forms or weapons forms, an hour of practice three times a week is the minimum for developing external and internal skill at these.

I still occasionally train with one of my former taiji instructors (in his mid-40s) who has retired from teaching and practices with partners only once or twice a year. In fighting terms, the only skill of his that seems a little rusty is his sense of control, not his tactics, timing, or short-power (fa-jing)!

However, the health benefits of form practice are not as cumulative, and regular practice is still essential, though the movements usually become smaller and "softer" in appearance of their own accord.

CONCLUSION

Any change in your own life-style, such as taking up a martial art, will effect changes in the lives of others as well. This may seem insignificant until you actually face the consequences. For example, your girlfriend may not understand why her birthday seems less important than the seminar scheduled on the same day; your family may not understand your sudden need to attend classes three days a week and fear that it will interfere with a "normal" life.

Studying an internal art can mean doing what you think is right for you even if others don't immediately understand or support you. However, few of us are Taoist monks living on qi and dew in a mountain cave; you also have to remember the need for compromise. For example, perhaps you can train two days a week at the club instead of three and do your home workouts in the early morning or late evening to minimize your time away from family.

On a personal level, you can't plan how you will react to changing circumstances. It is as futile as trying to train in and master techniques that cover every possible martial situation. That's why the internal arts, when taught and practiced properly, are so effective: they help the practitioner to learn principles and acquire skills for adapting to changing circumstances.

Learning to do this is difficult enough when it's a question of responding immediately to a martial tactic you've never experienced. It's even more difficult when you are faced with the emotional need to respond in an appropriate and spontaneous manner to an unexpected turn of events in your life.

Physical and mental preparation is the key to successful change in terms of learning and applying new martial skills, but even the most methodical preparation cannot banish all your fears and resistance to changing old habits.

At its most basic psychological level, accepting the need for change is difficult because it's easier to do things the way you are accustomed to doing them. For example, if you are used to the "block then strike" approach of most hard styles, the more relaxed, simultaneous counters of an internal art may seem impossible at first.

Learning to deal with change is a complex process, and, even without trying to make it happen, becoming relaxed, centered, and spontaneous on a physical level is bound to have similar ramifications for your emotional state and vice-versa.

Finally, developing a "real" understanding of all aspects of the internal arts is easy: find a competent instructor, follow his or her example and instruction, and, practice moderately and regularly for the rest of your life!

conclusion

It will take many years to master the techniques given in this book. Your diligence in practice will eventually show in movement and techniques that become more advanced.

The more you practice, the more you gain. Don't try to rush these techniques or go on to more advanced techniques before you've mastered the basics. Take it slowly and allow the forms to teach you. If you force the learning process, you will learn nothing.

Any student of taijiquan who has bothered to watch the students of other instructors or who has taken workshops with different instructors should be aware that the Yang style has changed a great deal since the days of Yang Ch'eng-fu and even more so when compared to the forms created by his grandfather, Yang Lu-ch'an.

Sadly, in most cases, the changes have not been for the better. Since the death of Ch'eng-fu in 1936, the majority of subsequent interpretations of the Yang slow and fast forms have lost much, if not all, of their health and combat benefits.

When you compare the forms taught by the handful of real masters presently alive to the majority of Yang styles being practiced around the world, it should be obvious that something has gone wrong in the process of transmission.

Sometimes this is deliberate, as when an expert changes the form to conceal its essence from the unworthy; however, more often the problem lies in the number and quality of the intermediaries between the student and whoever created the form/style being learned.

In general, the fewer people involved, the less chance there is of serious errors being introduced. Think of it like this—would you rather own the master recording of a symphony done with professional equipment or the copy you made from the bootleg copy somebody else made with amateur recording equipment?!

Traditionally, you were expected to learn a *complete* taiji curriculum for a minimum of 10 years before beginning to teach on your own. Nowadays, many instructors are teaching after learning only slow form and with just one or two years of instruction.

However, decades of practice do not necessarily bring greater depths of skill and insight. One of Michael's students, Marc Seguin, an auto mechanic, related to me how his favorite technical instructor asked, "Do you want to be someone who has learned for 10 years or someone who has done a year's worth of learning 10 times?"

It was a little easier in the "good old days" to know if a taiji instructor lacked real skill. The other instructors would visit periodically and offer, politely or otherwise, to beat the crap out of him. It's difficult to fake competence, even if it's only on a martial level, when someone is doing his best to throttle you!

It seems to be human nature to believe that you know it all, and changing your approach to the internal arts is not easy, especially if you do have some skill and have had competent instructors. After five years of training, you'll think you know it all; after 10 years you'll be amazed at how little you knew five years earlier!

Sadly, there are no magic answers in taiji or in life. Long-term effort, a willingness to change when change is necessary, and competent instruction are the keys to progress.

Good luck; we hope that this book has helped advance you a little way along that difficult but rewarding road.